D1592804

PASS CHRISTIAN

—— A N D · T H E ——

GAZEBO GAZETTE

PASS CHRISTIAN

AND THE

GAZEBO GAZETTE

A GULF COMMUNITY'S
POST-KATRINA TRIUMPH

LAWRENCE N. STROUT

THE
History
PRESS

Published by The History Press
Charleston, SC 29403
www.historypress.net

Front cover image courtesy of John Fleck/FEMA, September 27, 2005.

All images courtesy of the author unless otherwise noted.

First published 2015

Manufactured in the United States

ISBN 978.1.62619.093.1

Library of Congress Control Number: 2014953448

Notice: The information in this book is true and complete to the best of our knowledge. It is offered without guarantee on the part of the author or The History Press. The author and The History Press disclaim all liability in connection with the use of this book.

Dedicated to the memory of the twenty-eight Pass Christian men and women who died in Hurricane Katrina.

Hurricane Katrina Memorial located in Pass Christian's War Memorial Park.

CONTENTS

ACKNOWLEDGEMENTS

First, a special thanks goes to Pass Christian city officials and business leaders who generously made themselves available for interviews. Thanks to the University of Southern Mississippi Center for Oral History and Cultural Heritage and its director, Louis M. Kyriakoudes. Specifically, the center's Linda VanZandt provided some oral history transcripts by creating a DropBox folder, and Stephanie Millet went above and beyond the call of duty by e-mailing requested oral history transcripts directly to me. Many of the oral histories conducted under the Hurricane Katrina Oral History Project and Hurricane Katrina Pass Road to the Future were utilized thanks to Linda and Stephanie. Thanks to Ron Daley and Huey Bang for access to all their photographs of before and after Hurricane Katrina. Thanks to Doug Kyle of the U.S. Postal Service for photographs as well. Thanks to colleague Wendy Roussin, who created two photo illustrations of my home during Katrina and my home compared to the new flood elevation building levels. Thanks to Shawn Jerone, Pass Christian's "computer guy." Of course, thanks to my commissioning editor, who is now a senior commissioning editor, Christen Thompson, for all her help throughout the year and a half from when the contract was signed until the book was published.

Finally, to Evelina Shmukler Burnett, thanks for creating and publishing the *Gazebo Gazette* from January 2006 until June 2013. And to Jace Ponder, thanks for acquiring the *Gazette* and holding to its original community service principles while putting your own stamp on its look and content.

INTRODUCTION

On Sunday, August 28, 2005, my wife, Penny Rodrique; family friend Kelly Rouse; and I evacuated to the Celadon Beach Resort condominium complex on Panama City Beach in Florida, some 250 miles east and out of harm's way from Hurricane Katrina. We had a couple day's worth of clothes, but more importantly, virtually all our photographs and other sentimental items impossible to replace were stacked in our Dodge Grand Caravan. When Penny was seven years old, her family lost virtually everything they owned in Hurricane Camille, so Penny has but a few trinkets in a shoebox from her childhood. She was determined not to do that to her then twenty-three-year-old daughter, Nicole, who lived in Bloomington, Indiana.

At about 3:00 a.m. on Monday, August 29, I awoke and walked up to the television that had been left tuned to the Weather Channel. Katrina's massive eye was about to pass over the Mississippi Gulf Coast; you could see it clearly from the satellite image. I turned to my wife and said, "Our home will be gone." She replied without missing a beat, "My business..."

Let's be clear on one thing: we were among the lucky ones. Yes, we had seven feet of water in our home despite the fact that it stood on pilings seventeen and a half feet above sea level. Yes, my wife's four-thousand-square-foot metal building that housed her business, Mississippi Coast Fireworks, was destroyed, and a month after the storm, the Mississippi Department of Transportation took possession of the property under eminent domain as part of its rebuilding of the Bay of St. Louis Bridge on a new footprint. And yes, my office at Xavier University of Louisiana in New Orleans was flooded for days, wiping out research for a book I had started a decade before about a longtime Washington, D.C. reporter. But we *were* lucky. No relatives or close friends of ours were killed.

In the immediate days, months and years after Hurricane Katrina, I avoided mentally revisiting the storm and its devastating affects on Pass Christian, even though there were reminders all around. And despite years of experience as a journalist, there was no inclination to put on my "news" hat and start telling the story. When an event hits this close to home, personal survival takes precedence over professional interests. But from the early days of the *Gazebo Gazette*, I was fascinated at how a newspaper could be created organically (excuse the overused term) and evolve quickly into a necessity in the survival of Pass Christian. So this book is about the *Gazette* and Pass Christian residents' efforts to bring a city back. The book does not pretend to include the story of every person who played a major part in the Pass's resurrection, but it does intend to chronicle how many government and business leaders worked tirelessly so the city could survive and one day prosper again.

Chapter 1

PASS CHRISTIAN

The Calm Before the Storm

If you are on the Mississippi Gulf Coast and you do not evacuate, you will die.
—FOX 8, New Orleans meteorologist Bob Breck, Sunday morning,
August 28, 2005

B ob Breck arrived in New Orleans in 1978 after working for five years in Dayton, Ohio. While in New Orleans, he had forecast hurricanes, including Frederic (1979), Juan (1985), Andrew (1992), Georges (1998), Lilli (2002) and Ivan (2004). He was not known for hyperbole, so his evacuate or "you will die" warning got the Mississippi coast viewers' full attention. Breck pulled no punches about the potential for death and destruction, based partly on the New Orleans National Weather Service office statement from 10:11 a.m. on Sunday, August 28, 2005, that painted a grim picture about what was going to happen. The "urgent" weather message said that Katrina had "unprecedented strength" and that after landfall, "most of the area will be uninhabitable for weeks…perhaps longer." But the "urgent" message did not stop there. It said that "airborne debris will be widespread…and may include heavy items such as household appliances and even light vehicles" and that "persons…pets…and livestock exposed to the winds will face certain death if struck." The "urgent" message predicted: "Power outages will last for weeks…as most power poles will be down and transformers destroyed. Water shortages will make human suffering incredible by modern standards."[1]

When Hurricane Katrina hit, the population of Pass Christian, Mississippi, was 6,655, with about 65 percent white, 28 percent African American, 4 percent Vietnamese and 2 percent Hispanic.[2] The self-proclaimed birthplace

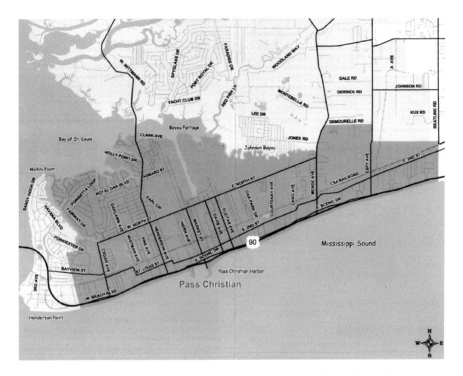

Map of Pass Christian. The Mississippi Sound, Bay of St. Louis and Bayou Portage border the city on three sides. *Courtesy of Gulf Regional Planning Commission and the City of Pass Christian.*

of yachting in the South, the Pass—as it is known to the locals—lies about 55.0 miles east-northeast of New Orleans on the Mississippi Gulf Coast. The city itself is only 8.4 square miles and 6.0 miles at its widest point, but it also includes 6.9 square miles of water.[3] The most important geographic characteristic to the Pass's story about Hurricane Katrina is that the city is a peninsula, surrounded by water essentially on three sides: the Mississippi Sound to the south, the Bay of St. Louis to the west and the Bayou Portage to the northwest.

According to the Pass Christian Historical Society, the Choctaw roamed the area before Europeans arrived in 1699, when Pierre Le Moyne D'Iberville claimed the coast for France. The coast bounced from France to England and then to Spain before it became territory of the United States in 1810. Even before Pass Christian was officially chartered as a town in 1838, a lighthouse was built, and the Pass Christian Hotel opened in 1831. The city has a long history as a summer-home destination with an unmistakable link to New Orleans. As early as the 1840s—as the historical society notes—

the Pass's beachfront property was being acquired by New Orleanians for weekend retreats. City officials estimate that as many as 30 percent of the homes in the Pass before Hurricane Katrina were second homes, mostly of people who lived in New Orleans. Scenic Drive is well known among preservationists in the country. The street parallels Highway 90 and features homes built in the nineteenth century. Scenic is one of a handful of sites in the United States that is designated as a national historic street, and the National Trust for Historic Preservation called it "one of the largest architecturally intact historic areas in the South."[4]

In 1969, Pass Christian was where Hurricane Camille's eye passed onto land. The hurricane struck on August 17, killed 143 on the Mississippi Gulf Coast alone (another 113 due to inland flooding) and featured wind strength peaking at about 175 miles per hour.[5] From the year 1900 until now, Hurricane Camille remains second only to the Florida Keys Labor Day hurricane in 1935 in maximum sustained winds. Hurricane Camille forever changed not only the lives of those in Pass Christian and other towns on the coast but also forecasting. The consensus was that the warnings issued for Camille were inadequate. One of the ways that deficiency was addressed was the creation of the Saffir-Simpson Hurricane Wind Scale of a 1 to 5 categorization based on the intensity of the storm. Camille would eventually be slotted in as a Category 5—the most powerful—which includes storms with sustained winds exceeding 157 miles per hour. And from the day after Hurricane Camille made landfall through Pass Christian, August 17 became the date to which all future life events were linked for its residents. So on the day before Hurricane Katrina's landfall about thirty-six years after Camille, Pass Christian residents were comforted by the matter-of-fact (but misguided) belief that nothing could be worse than Camille.

In fact, less than thirty-six hours before Hurricane Katrina made landfall, people who would ultimately end up rebuilding Pass Christian—either in the public sector as leaders or as business owners who decided to invest in the community and return—had no idea what was about to take place or how their lives were about to change. But not one of them would ever forget what they were doing—whether evacuating or hunkering down—in those final hours before Katrina.

For Pass Christian city officials—elected and appointed—some stayed in the city by choice and others by necessity. Still others evacuated with most of the rest of the citizenry. Alderman Leo "Chipper" McDermott spent his entire life in the Pass, except for his college years at the University of Southern Mississippi in Hattiesburg, about ninety miles to the north.

McDermott's home is located in the eastern portion of Pass Christian, the highest ground in the city. So, as he had in previous storms, McDermott stayed in the city for Hurricane Katrina, looking after his ninety-three-year-old aunt, who lived just across the street from his home. McDermott, under circumstances that were wholly related to Hurricane Katrina, would end up saddled with a seemingly insurmountable task that his grandfather (Dr. J.H. Spence) had not faced as mayor in the century before.

Ward 3 alderman Anthony Hall wore more than one hat in the city of Pass Christian. While he was elected to his first full term on the board of aldermen in 2005, Hall's full-time job was running the Long Beach/Pass Christian Wastewater Treatment Plant on Fleitas Avenue. The treatment plant has generators and a two-story storm-rated building. So without hesitation, Hall and his wife, son and daughter decided to take supplies from their home to the treatment plant and ride out the storm. At about 7:00 p.m. the night before the storm's landfall, the Halls arrived at the treatment plant. Hall's wife and children eventually fell asleep while Hall held vigil over the plant.

Malcolm Jones and his then wife, Theresa, a local dentist, made a deal when they decided to build a multimillion-dollar, 6,800-square-foot home on historic Scenic Drive directly off the beach: evacuate if there was any chance of danger from an oncoming hurricane. So Jones, a divorce attorney and on-again, off-again city attorney; his wife; and the two of his four daughters who were still living at home traveled to Vicksburg, where his in-laws lived, on Saturday to ride out the storm.

Police chief John Dubuisson is a Pass Christian lifer. Born in nearby Gulfport, where the closest hospital is located, he graduated from Pass High School; served in the army, including a stint in Vietnam; and then enrolled in the Mississippi Law Enforcement Officers Training Academy to become a police officer. Dubuisson started as a patrolman and worked his way up to chief in the mid-1980s. Unlike residents who faced mandatory evacuation orders as Hurricane Katrina bore down on the coast, the Pass Christian emergency plan called for the chief and a skeleton crew to remain in the city during the storm. City hall, located on Scenic Drive, and the Pass Christian Public Library right behind city hall to the north were selected as emergency headquarters because the buildings were located on ground declared "high and safe."

Kathryn "Sally" James, the longtime Pass Christian librarian, admittedly had no plan as Hurricane Katrina neared the coast. Finally, on the Saturday night before the Monday landfall of the storm, James decided to make reservations at a motel just north of Mobile, Alabama. At about 11:00 a.m.

on Sunday, she set out for the motel on a drive that normally would have taken about an hour and a half. James arrived at her accommodations five and a half hours after hitting the road. Interstate 10 was jammed with cars filled with families fleeing both New Orleans to the west and the entire Mississippi Gulf Coast.

Marsha Garziano joined the Pass Christian School District in 1986 as business manager. Fully cognizant that a major storm was about to hit, she spent Saturday doing the end-of-the-month payroll and making night drops into the local banks so regardless of whether the schools opened right after the storm, teachers and other employees would be paid. Garziano also took some of the district's key documents and financial records from the leased Davis Avenue administration building and packed them up on the second floor of the Pass Christian High School. At each school in the district, administrators picked up everything valuable off the floors to prevent possible water damage from leaky roofs or flooding. Despite the fact that Garziano's home was on Eleanor Avenue—again located on the east side of town, considered very high ground—she evacuated north near Wiggins with relatives.

Pass Christian business owners also had decisions to make with a killer storm bearing down on the coast. Bruce Anthony was raised in Pass Christian, and after a long career as a project manager with BellSouth in Alabama, he retired in 1991 and moved back to work in his brother's business, Wastewater Plant Service Company, or WPSCO. Anthony had experience with the aftermath of a large hurricane, having returned to the Pass for a month after Hurricane Camille to help his brother, father and uncle get the sewer and water system back up and running. On Hurricane Katrina's eve, Anthony strategically placed major WPSCO construction equipment on vacant land at the corner of Clarke Avenue and Second Street, theoretically safe ground and close to where it would be used. Several of the company's pickup-sized trucks were parked at Anthony's home north of Second Street on Eleanor, thirty feet above sea level. Anthony's wife evacuated, but he stayed in his home after boarding up all the windows, ready to spring into action coordinating any repairs to the sewer and water system that might be needed after the hurricane.

George Schloegel—president of Hancock Bank, which operates about 160 locations on the coasts of Florida, Alabama, Mississippi and Louisiana—had started in motion the bank's "disaster recovery" plans well before the weekend leading up to Hurricane Katrina. Schloegel, using the multistory Hancock Bank Building in downtown Gulfport as a central headquarters, oversaw all of the banks' procedures for safeguarding customer records; he also prepared each branch, many of which were in harm's way at low elevations, for the worst. But while preparing for the worst, Schloegel did not for one second think Hurricane Katrina would be anything like Hurricane Camille. In fact, in a late Sunday night interview with Fox News, Schloegel was asked how he thought Katrina was comparing to Camille. He said, "Well, I was here during Camille, and I'm here during Katrina, and this doesn't look like Camille to me."[6] Meanwhile, the Hancock Bank Building in Pass Christian was boarded up, and all records and movable electronics were moved upstairs. The building dates back to 1928, when the downstairs was for bank business and the upstairs was a doctor's office and a telephone company office. The bank's presence, though, dates way back to 1902, when Pass Christian became the location of the second branch of Hancock Bank, which was founded in 1899. For all previous storms, the seventy-seven-year-old bank building was on high enough ground to survive without any flooding.

Real estate broker and owner of Mississippi Coast Realty Ken Austin told friends who decided to evacuate on the Saturday before the storm that they were overreacting. Initially, Austin decided to stay at his home on Fairway Drive in the low-lying middle-class Timber Ridge subdivision. But Austin was awakened by friends sometime after midnight Saturday and informed that the storm had taken a turn for the worse and was now Category 5, the most powerful designation. He quickly decided to secure his real estate office one block from the beach at the corner of Henderson Avenue and St. Louis Street as best he could—wrapping three desktop computers tightly in plastic to prevent any possible leaks in the roof from destroying them. Smartly, though, Austin took files and financial records with him and felt secure because he was utilizing online backup services to guard against losing all his company's data. When the sun came up on Sunday, Austin boarded up his house and headed to the home of Linda Wallace, a friend who lived north on Menge Avenue in a subdivision called Byrnewood. Austin escaped in his 1997 Chevrolet pickup truck and left his new car in his home's garage to protect it from falling trees and debris.

Tommy Allison opened his C&J Quick Stop convenience store and gas station in July 1999. The station is located at the corner of Henderson Avenue and North Street. On the Sunday before Katrina's arrival, the Pass Christian Police and Fire Departments asked Allison how late he would be willing to stay open before evacuating. Allison set 3:00 p.m. as the latest he could stay, and right before he closed, the Pass Christian Police Department topped off the gasoline tanks in its patrol cars. Allison did not board up or do any other storm preparation at his gas station or his home in Timber Ridge. He simply got in his truck and evacuated to relatives north in nearby Picayune.

Upon graduating from high school in 1980, Mike LaMarca Jr. attended one year of college in Monroe, Louisiana. When he returned home in May 1981, his father had just purchased a restaurant, Pirate's Cove. The younger LaMarca worked in his father's restaurant that summer, and his education from that point on was "on the job"—he never returned to college. Pirate's Cove restaurant established a reputation for serving the best po'boys in the region. Located on historic Highway 90, Mike LaMarca Jr. took over running the restaurant after his father retired in 2002. On the weekend before Hurricane Katrina, LaMarca closed Pirate's Cove on Saturday around midday and boarded up the restaurant's windows as pretty much a standard operating procedure to prevent flying debris from causing major damage. LaMarca and his wife, Dawn, toyed with the idea of staying in their home located about one and a half miles off the beach. But their children became scared, so on Sunday, the family packed up and drove to Dawn's sister and brother-in-law's home about four or five miles north of Interstate 10. The location was perfect: almost certainly out of harm's way but close enough so that after the storm the LaMarcas could make their way back to the Pass quickly to check on their business and home.

Southern Printing and Silkscreening was founded in 1972 in the garage of Homer Jenkins. Jenkins, a former University of Colorado football star who went on to play for the Hamilton Tiger Cats of the Canadian Football League, expanded the business over the years, and since the late 1990s, it has been located on Davis Avenue. Four of Homer's sons—Perry, Mark, Brent and Dane—took over when Homer retired before Hurricane Katrina. As Katrina moved closer to the Mississippi Gulf Coast, Perry Jenkins, who serves as manager of the business, was not the least bit worried. He had lived through Hurricane Camille hunkered down in St. Paul Elementary School, which had served as a shelter. Standard operating procedure called for the Jenkinses to cover all computers and large equipment to guard against damage caused by any leaks in the roof. Perry didn't even board up his home, located near the business on St. Paul Avenue, but his family evacuated to the Florida panhandle. As a volunteer firefighter, Perry Jenkins joined eight to ten other firefighters at the East End fire station on Second Street to ride out the storm.

Dr. Jennifer Hendrick, owner of Live Oak Animal Hospital, was enjoying her first $1 million billing year and contemplating hiring a full-time associate to expand what was her single-doctor veterinary practice. As Hurricane Katrina approached the coast, her first thought was to stay. Hendrick had obligations that others did not; she had dogs and cats at her hospital that she felt responsible for. But on Sunday, it became apparent that this was not just another "mild" hurricane. Hendrick and her boyfriend, Scott Niolet (they have since married), packed their Cadillac Escalade with nine dogs—their dogs and others from the hospital—and headed east with the ultimate intent to go to north Alabama. The drive was slow and tedious, as evacuees were all headed in the same direction. That Sunday night, Niolet pulled the Escalade over on the side of the road in Dothan, Alabama, and he and Hendrick slept in the back of the vehicle with all nine dogs. As they went to sleep that night, Hendrick could not help but think about the few animals that could not travel. Those animals were left in the highest location possible in her hospital, which was one block from the beach on St. Louis Street in a renovated building that had once been the city's post office.

The "new" Pass Christian Post Office was located inland on the northern side of the railroad tracks on Davis Avenue. Postmaster Pete McGoey toyed with the idea of staying at the post office, keeping in mind the postal service's policy that the mail should be delivered the next day after a storm if at all possible. Instead, McGoey left his post office after he and his crew made sure that all electronic equipment, such as computers, were not left on the floor in case water somehow got into the building. McGoey decided to stay in his rented house in Long Beach, some six miles from the Pass Christian post office.

The city's clergy also had decisions to make on the eve of the storm. Father Christopher Colby was the pastor of Pass Christian's Trinity Episcopal Church, which lies on a prime piece of property filled with centuries-old oak trees that borders Highway 90. As the son of a navy dentist and a man of the cloth, Colby was all too familiar with moving around throughout the country. In 1997, after becoming sick of moving, Colby settled in Pass Christian. On Sunday morning, the day before Hurricane Katrina's landfall, Colby felt doomed. Without the benefit of an adequate hurricane plan for Trinity Church, Colby packed up two boxes of church records and placed them in an upstairs hall of his home. After performing a Sunday morning service to seven people who had not yet evacuated, Colby packed up his car with suitcases filled with three changes of clothes, and he, his wife, mother-in-law and dog headed for a hotel in Mobile, Alabama. Before he left, he gently placed the altar cross from Trinity Church in the trunk of his car for safekeeping. Meanwhile, parishioners of another church, St. Paul Catholic

Church, felt confident that whatever the strength Katrina was at landfall, their A-framed metal church, unlike any other Catholic church in the world, would survive. Up until Hurricane Camille in 1969, St. Paul's parish attended a church built in the mid-nineteenth century. Camille destroyed that church, which was located on historic Scenic Drive. In its place, a so-called slip-and-slide-looking church, whose metal roof could be seen for miles off the coast by commercial fishermen and recreational boaters, was erected. On his way out of the city to safe ground, Father Dennis Carver handed the key to St. Paul Elementary School to Chief John Dubuisson. Carver reasoned that the school could be used by the city as a safe haven after the storm for residents who decided not to evacuate.

While Trinity and St. Paul's had had a presence in the Pass since the mid-1800s, First Baptist Church on Second Street didn't arrive until 1929. The church had a small congregation, but unlike Trinity and St. Paul's, it was located on slightly higher ground and one block inland, helping it to survive Hurricane Camille when Trinity, St. Paul's and many other buildings in Pass Christian did not. Pastor Bill Smith and his wife, Carolyn, had come to the coast as retirees of the Southern Baptist Convention in 1995 after serving the church in various locations overseas. In 2000, the First Baptist Church lured Smith out of retirement to become its pastor. The Smiths lived in a nearby Long Beach home that had survived Hurricane Camille. So the Smiths huddled at their home on the Sunday before Katrina to ride out the storm. Carolyn Smith wasn't the least bit worried.

And there were individuals who were not in the Pass but who were drawn to this coastal community in the months and years after Hurricane Katrina. Long Beach native Adam Pace was in Hattiesburg attending the University of Southern Mississippi as an architectural engineering major. Pace is a graduate of St. Stanislaus in Bay St. Louis. He remembers the first day as a seventh-grader befriending Ben Puckett Jr. of Pass Christian; they were best friends through all of high school. Pace hung out at Puckett's home and at Martin Hardware in downtown Pass Christian throughout his high school years. But when Hurricane Katrina came ashore, Pace was safely in Hattiesburg, though he missed the coast and felt out of sorts away from it.

Margaret Loesch, the daughter of Brigadier General L.F. Loesch, lived all over the world while a historic home on Scenic Drive served as her family's vacation getaway. Loesch remembers spending every summer and most holidays on the coast restoring the home that had been built in the 1840s. Her father sold that house after Hurricane Camille, and when her father died in a plane crash, Loesch and her mother and brother moved to the coast permanently and lived in the so-called Ewing House, also on Scenic Drive. After going to school on the coast and earning degrees from the University of Southern Mississippi and the University of New Orleans, Loesch moved to California and, years later, went on to create and/or produce some of the most iconic characters and shows in TV history. *The Smurfs, G.I. Joe, Transformers, Muppet Babies, Power Rangers, Bobby's World* and *X-Men* were just some of the shows Loesch was intimately involved with over the years. Even after Loesch left Pass Christian for Hollywood, she remembered as a child idealizing and dreaming about the Pass. As a twenty-three-year-old in 1969, Loesch remembered Hurricane Camille and its devastation, despite the fact that her family home survived relatively unscathed. Over the years, Loesch wanted to buy back that family vacation home but never had the means to do so. It was no wonder, then, that as Hurricane Katrina headed for the Mississippi Gulf Coast, Loesch tracked the hurricane on the news from her home in Los Angeles. From afar, Loesch had a feeling that Hurricane Katrina was going to be another Hurricane Camille.

Also on that weekend leading up to landfall, without a full-time job, Evelina Shmukler sat in her parents' home in Atlanta, Georgia, wondering whether journalism would continue to be her career choice. Shmukler had never visited the Mississippi Gulf Coast, much less ever heard of Pass Christian. The Ukrainian-born Columbia University journalism graduate who had traveled the world covering stories for the *Wall Street Journal* and the Dow Jones Newswire would quite by chance end up on the coast covering the storm and then, as the weeks and months passed, in Pass Christian as a volunteer. Unbeknownst to Evelina Shmukler, Hurricane Katrina was about to change her entire life.

Chapter 2

HURRICANE KATRINA

The Struggle for Survival

[Hurricane] *Camille compared to this one* [Hurricane Katrina]
was a thunderstorm.
—*Police chief John Dubuisson*

John Dubuisson was one of the first to learn that Hurricane Katrina would redefine "high ground" in Pass Christian and the coast. When the water rose beyond anyone's expectations, the chief and twelve police officers and firefighters had to hop from city hall to the Pass Christian Public Library—one of the city's highest points—to seek safety. Assuming the area was "high ground," people had parked their cars around the buildings but to no use; one by one, the cars were swept away as the surge came in. Dubuisson, his officers and the firefighters watched as car after car passed by the library, missing the Category 3 storm glass double doors that were the only thing that kept the water from flowing in. But as luck would have it this day, the final car seemed to have a magnet for the front doors. It crashed into the doors, not breaking the glass, but opening the doors enough so the water started filling the library. Officers jumped up on anything they could to get out of the water flow. If the back doors could not be breached, all thirteen would drown in the library, which had concrete walls and a concrete ceiling. They shot twenty or more rounds with their .45-caliber handguns at the back door storm glass windows to try to let the water out. The glass proved to be bulletproof; the windows did not break. Dubuisson waded in the strong current to open the back doors, knowing he would be swept out by the surge. Maybe, he thought, he would be able to grab a railing just on

Pass Christian City Hall was destroyed by Hurricane Katrina's surge despite being located on what was considered "high" ground. *Courtesy of Mark Wolfe/FEMA, September 14, 2005.*

Two Pass Christian Police Department cruisers landed in the historic Live Oak Cemetery. *Courtesy of the Department of Defense, September 12, 2005.*

the other side of the double doors or perhaps seek refuge by swimming to an oak tree about twenty-five yards from the library. He opened the door and was slammed into the railing. His head just above the water, he held on for dear life just long enough for the building to empty and the flow to become somewhat manageable. Officers and firefighters grabbed a telephone line to steady them and walked through the powerful surge to climb up onto the roof of the library to safety. One of Dubuisson's officers in the library, Michael Lally Jr., called Katrina's surge "awe inspiring" and admitted that Mother Nature on that day made him feel "insignificant."[7]

The GeoResources Institute at Mississippi State University ascertained that the high-water mark for Hurricane Katrina's surge in Pass Christian was 28.0 feet above sea level compared to Hurricane Camille's 23.4 feet, recorded by the U.S. Geological Survey. The surge was not the only way Katrina was more destructive than Camille. While Camille was two categories higher and had maximum sustained winds almost 38 percent stronger when it hit the Mississippi Gulf Coast, Katrina's hurricane-force winds extended 120 miles from the storm center as compared to Camille, whose winds extended only 60. Furthermore, Katrina's eye was large—37 miles—as opposed to Camille's eye, which was 11. In Pass Christian alone, 28 residents died. A total of 238 people died in Mississippi and 1,833 in Alabama, Florida, Georgia, Louisiana and Mississippi combined, according to the National Hurricane Center (NHC).[8] And even though Camille claimed 78 lives in Pass Christian alone, it was no surprise that the NHC final report called Katrina "one of the most devastating natural disasters in United States' history" and the deadliest hurricane in seventy-seven years. The NHC described perfectly what many cities on the coast experienced: "The storm surge of Katrina struck the Mississippi coastline with such ferocity that entire coastal communities were obliterated, some left with little more than foundations upon which homes, businesses, government facilities and other historical buildings once stood."[9] Illustrating just how bad the destruction and debris field was in Pass Christian, it wasn't until as late as the last weekend in October—two full months after Hurricane Katrina—that a debris removal crew discovered a body, missed by the government rescue and recovery effort, buried in the rubble.

Hurricane Katrina "took us from the twenty-first century to the eighteenth century in six hours," Pass Christian mayor Chipper McDermott has said more than once over the years. Specifically, about 80 to 85 percent of the homes were gone (washed out to the Mississippi Sound), destroyed with only rubble remaining or were uninhabitable (at least the frame remaining and

Satellite photograph of Hurricane Katrina lurking in the Gulf. *Courtesy of the National Oceanic and Atmospheric Administration.*

Two unidentified people walking over debris covering the street. *Courtesy of Huey Bang.*

rebuildable) because of the winds and unprecedented surge. That left about 350 to 400 of the 2,600 homes—which about 1,000 people lived in—as livable, largely in the easternmost portion of the city, but most of them did not have power or water and sewer service. Most people had evacuated because the first head count of people in the city the day after the storm, done by a door-to-door search, tallied only 178 people.[10] Further, 96 to 98 percent of the businesses were destroyed.

In fact, damage to public and commercial buildings, businesses and churches in Pass Christian by Hurricane Katrina included:

- city hall, destroyed
- police department headquarters, destroyed
- fire department West End station, destroyed
- fire department East End station, flooded four feet but habitable
- public library, destroyed
- old library, built circa 1853 and recently restored, gone
- elementary school, destroyed
- middle school, destroyed
- high school, uninhabitable
- J.W. Randolph School, built in 1928 to educate African Americans, uninhabitable
- St. Paul Elementary School, uninhabitable
- St. Paul Catholic Church, uninhabitable
- Our Mother of Mercy Catholic Church, uninhabitable
- Trinity Episcopal Church, uninhabitable
- First Missionary Baptist Church, destroyed
- First Baptist Church, destroyed
- Goodwill Missionary Baptist Church, destroyed
- chamber of commerce, gone
- U.S. Post Office, destroyed
- Boys and Girls Club, destroyed
- Dixie White House, uninhabitable
- historical society, gone, except for an old bank vault
- Union House, historical Civil War structure, uninhabitable
- Miramar Lodge Nursing Home, a 182-bed facility, destroyed
- Twin Oaks Assisted Living, destroyed
- Walmart, destroyed
- Winn-Dixie/Rite Aid strip mall, gone
- Peoples Bank, gone, except for the main bank vault

- Hancock Bank, uninhabitable
- Pass Christian Yacht Club, gone
- Pass Christian Harbor, destroyed
- Family Dollar, uninhabitable
- Palace in the Pass, gone
- McDonald's, gone
- Pirate's Cove restaurant, gone
- Harbor View Café, gone
- Domino's Pizza, gone
- Tigres restaurant, gone
- Harbor Oaks Inn, gone
- Blue Rose, historic bed-and-breakfast, uninhabitable
- Hillyer House, art gallery and gift shop, destroyed
- Pass Christian Isles Golf Club, destroyed
- C&J Quick Stop gas station, uninhabitable
- Russell's Service Station, destroyed
- BP gas station, gone
- Martin Hardware, destroyed
- Pass Books, gone
- Live Oak Animal Hospital, gone
- Colonnade Office Building, uninhabitable
- C.C. Lynch Building, uninhabitable
- Southern Printing and Silkscreening, uninhabitable
- Adolph Bourdin Air Conditioning & Heating, uninhabitable

The saddest part is that this list is not comprehensive but rather a partial accounting of the destruction that any resident would be able to list off the top of his or her head.

Hurricane Katrina cut off Pass Christian from the rest of the world. To the immediate west, the Bay of St. Louis Bridge on scenic Highway 90 was destroyed. In fact, Highway 90, which is also the main east–west travel route for the coastal cities, was impassable all the way from the Bay Bridge in the west to the Biloxi Bay Bridge to the east. The main three ways that residents could return to Pass Christian were from the north: Henderson, Menge and Espy Avenues.

Chief John Dubuisson moved from the library's roof, where he and twelve other men had sought refuge from the surge, to the second floor of St. Paul Elementary School and then to the East End fire station on Second Street, where he spent the night. Specifically, Dubuisson stretched out on

The destroyed Bay of St. Louis Bridge on Highway 90. The bridge connects Pass Christian with Bay St. Louis. *Courtesy of John Fleck/FEMA, October 4, 2005.*

the back of a fire truck looking at the sky. He remembers how bright the stars looked without any lights on for miles on the coast and how quiet it was. Dubuisson noted the silence; not even any crickets had survived the storm. Besides worrying about his department and the safety of everyone in the city, Dubuisson also had to deal with the personal side. His Market Street home, with one payment left on the mortgage, had floated off its piers and landed awkwardly on a utility pole. It was not salvageable. More importantly, he had left his two dogs on the back porch with the gate open, giving them access to a fenced yard. He assumed that they died in the storm. However, miraculously, three days after the storm, he discovered that both somehow survived, though one of them had to be chased for the better part of an hour to catch him because he was in shock. It was, finally, some good news for the chief.

The day after the storm, Tommy Allison traveled from his evacuation point in Picayune south to his Shell gas station at the corner of Henderson Avenue and North Street. He confirmed that gas remained untainted in the underground tanks at his station. On Thursday, he loaded up several empty fifty-gallon barrels, a generator and a pump and again traveled to his Shell station. By that time, Pass Christian police had set up a tent under the canopy of the gas station and operated the property as a central police station. The Shell station was selected primarily because it was where the only gasoline in the city was located. So Allison filled the tanks of the police and fire department vehicles that survived. Just as he filled his barrels, a FEMA representative introduced himself and informed Allison that FEMA needed the pump and the station's tanks for the rescue and recovery effort. Over the next couple of days, FEMA brought in a number of trailers, including one devoted solely to medical care. Military fuel tankers brought in fuel, filling the tanks of the once thriving gas station to be used for emergency operations only. Next to the Shell, a vacant Family Dollar store parking lot had become a helicopter pad where FEMA could fly in food and water to distribute through various points of distribution (PODS).

When listening to the radio after the storm in Vicksburg, city attorney Malcolm Jones gained his first inkling of just how bad Hurricane Katrina had damaged the coast. With the power out in Vicksburg, Jones listened to his car radio to try to find out what was going on. Jones heard Governor Haley Barbour address Mississippi citizens about the storm, and Barbour's voice was cracking. He could hear the governor crying. Jones knew Barbour as an unflappable politician, a dynamo in the Republican Party and former

Police dispatcher Gloria Sanders's home floated north and landed at the Shell station on the corner of North Street and Henderson Avenue. *Courtesy of Second Lieutenant Murray B. Shugars, Mississippi National Guard, September 12, 2005.*

chairman of the Republican National Committee. If Barbour is reduced to tears, Jones thought, things are bad.

When Jones returned to Pass Christian on Wednesday, he observed people walking aimlessly around. Police and firefighters had essentially been working day and night. There was plenty of manpower but "no tools." It turned out that even though his home survived, sixty-nine-year-old Mayor Billy McDonald, who was elected first in 1995, was, according to Jones, "not engaged" and seemed to be in shock. In large part, the police and firefighters were doing what they could on foot because most of the police and fire department vehicles were destroyed. Chief Dubuisson observed that people were in "shock, disbelief, despair" even days after the storm, asking no one in particular, "Where do we go from here?" Dubuisson said they were looking for leadership or someone in charge. The chief, who was nineteen years old when Hurricane Camille came ashore, immediately identified stark differences between Camille and Hurricane Katrina. Dubuisson said that after Camille, there were buildings and structures left in the city, even on the beachfront. But after Katrina, Dubuisson observed, nothing was left: "This time it's like you take a pencil and eraser and just erased every home. It's not there anymore; it's just naked property."[11]

As Alderman Anthony Hall's family slept on Sunday night into Monday morning at the wastewater treatment facility that he managed, water kept rising. The surge that inundated the treatment plant came from the north and Bayou Portage, not from the beach. On Monday afternoon, the surge receded, so Hall and his family could leave the plant and survey the damage. Both cars had been under water, so the Halls walked about four blocks to their home, which had floated off its pilings and was twisted but still secure with all their belongings inside. With essential duties as the plant manager and additionally as an alderman, Hall eventually got his wife and children north to his older brother's house in DeLisle before returning to the Pass and taking on the challenge of getting the city back on its feet.

Even before the water started breaking through the levees in New Orleans, Margaret Loesch, sitting in her Los Angeles home, knew Pass Christian was in trouble. After all, despite the fact that she had been in Hollywood for decades, she had lived through Hurricane Camille in a historic home on Scenic Drive in the Pass. Forty-eight hours after the storm, Loesch hopped on a plane from Los Angeles to Jackson, Mississippi, meeting a cousin from Chicago she had recruited. Loesch rented an SUV, drove to the local Walmart and stocked it with everything imaginable that hurricane survivors would need, including water, clothes, cleaning supplies, first aid kits, flashlights, batteries and the like. When she arrived on the coast the day after she landed in Jackson, she was not prepared for what she describes as a "four-day marathon of no sleep" trying to get the thousands of dollars' worth of supplies to those who needed them. While trying to convince the National Guard to allow her to deliver the supplies, Loesch consoled a woman who was distraught because she was not allowed back into the city to view her home. Of all the residents trying to return to survey property, this woman and her husband's home, coincidentally, was the childhood summer home of Loesch. With the "new" owners in tow, Loesch eluded the National Guard and promptly flagged down a sheriff's car. The deputy escorted her to the Pass Christian East End fire station, where the supplies were much appreciated. Immediately, Loesch traveled to look at how her childhood home had weathered the storm. The first glance of the home was "gut-wrenching," and to a casual observer, it was hard to ascertain whether this historic home was salvageable.[12]

In the immediate aftermath of the storm, difficult and unpopular decisions were made under the umbrella of the public good. With the mayor incapacitated and the aldermen part time, Malcolm Jones sprang into action, and the aldermen changed his title from city attorney to chief administrative assistant at their first official meeting after the storm on September 5. With the police department and FEMA all set up at the North Street Shell station, and the city government's initial command post set up at the Abbey Road

A delegation of U.S. senators views the devastation with Pass Christian's chief administrative assistant/city attorney Malcolm Jones. *Courtesy of Mark Wolfe/FEMA, September 16, 2005.*

Athletic Club off Menge Avenue, the main problems during the initial search and rescue and in the later days of recovery were dangerous mounds of debris everywhere and people quickly filtering into the city to steal and loot property. First, Jones and the city aldermen closed the city; people who had stayed and survived in livable homes could remain, but no one else was allowed in. Roadblocks were set up on the main roads coming from the north—Henderson, Menge and Espy Avenues. The east–west historic Highway 90 was impassable, deeming a roadblock unnecessary. This early decision frustrated residents. Each day, citizens would congregate at the Abbey Road command post hoping to secure passes so that they could go view their properties and salvage whatever might be left. It wasn't until September 13, 2005—two weeks after Hurricane Katrina made landfall—that residents were allowed back into Pass Christian, and even then, it was under a curfew for most of the city. On the few passable roads into the city, officials handed residents fliers that said, "You enter at your own risk" and warned them of mental health hazards associated with returning to a city whose landmarks were nearly all gone.

Debris removal decisions were made three days after residents were allowed to return to the most devastated parts of Pass Christian. Jones recommended and the aldermen approved hiring the Army Corps of Engineers and letting it do the subcontracting as well as deal with FEMA. This was instead of seeking money from FEMA and then contracting with a company for debris removal or vice versa. With the Army Corps handed the job, Pass Christian would not have to bureaucratically seek money from the government to pay for it. So the Army Corps dealt directly with FEMA. The Army Corps hired AshBritt, Inc., a Florida firm, and quickly debris removal began. Other than complaints that AshBritt did not subcontract enough with local area truckers—which became a major complaint from some— the problem of clearing private property without the owners' permission was a major issue. During a September visit to Pass Christian by President George W. Bush, Jones broached the subject of removing debris from private property without an owner's permission. The president turned to an aide, who responded that removing it without an owner's permission was a delicate subject. Jones chimed in that he had read the Robert T. Stafford Disaster Relief and Emergency Assistance Act of 1988 the night before and that under "catastrophic" conditions an executive order could be issued to remove the debris from private property if it would "eliminate immediate threats to life, public health and safety" and "ensure economic recovery of the affected community to the benefit of the community at large."[13] Bush turned to his aide and said, "Is that so?" No sooner had the aide nodded "yes" than Bush turned to Jones and said go ahead.

WPSCO's Bruce Anthony's home, in the eastern portion of the city, lost shingles and nearly lost its roof, but it remained livable. With the debris line just one hundred yards south of his home, Anthony knew things were going to be horrific downtown. Quickly, he made his way to the corner of Clarke Avenue and Second Street and found that $1.5 million worth of equipment that had been parked there on "safe" ground was destroyed. The state health department quickly arrived in the city and gave Anthony and city engineer John Campton an ultimatum: get water and sewer services to the livable homes ASAP or the city would be closed down. So, another reasonably quick and somewhat controversial decision was made. Knowing that it would be years before new permanent water and sewer lines could be run, Campton designed a temporary system with pipes run on top of the ground, which was approved by Jones and the aldermen as there was no other alternative. That action helped save the remaining population from being evicted due to unsanitary conditions. Alderman Anthony Hall, whose Ward 3 was largely destroyed, called the decision simply "common sense," but some residents felt the eastern homes in the Pass got preferential treatment when there were greater needs elsewhere.

Debris removal in Pass Christian by AshBritt, Inc., overseen by the Army Corps of Engineers. *Courtesy of Mike Wolfe/FEMA, December 21, 2005.*

FEMA provided food tents at Fleitas Avenue near War Memorial Park and in the parking lot of the former middle school at the corner of Church Avenue and St. Louis Street across from what remained of the Trinity Episcopal Church. Just to the west of Trinity, Ken Austin learned that his Mississippi Coast Realty office, located one block from the beach, was gone. Then, a quick check of his home in Timber Ridge confirmed what he had heard about the neighborhood: his home and the brand-new car he had parked in the garage to protect it from falling trees had been submerged in over twenty feet of water. Not prone to wallow in dismay, Austin traveled to Dallas and then Houston in the weeks following Katrina. With his home uninhabitable and having a strong desire to return to the Pass, Austin bought an RV in Houston and drove it to a friend's driveway on Abbey Road (near the city's initial command post), where he lived for the next nine months. While the city aldermen and Jones were holding public meetings regularly at the East End fire station, Austin recalled that it was the FEMA food tents that literally and figuratively "fed our community." Austin said that these FEMA locations served as places where people could reconnect. The food tents were where residents learned of the fate of neighbors and friends, as well as what was going on in the city. Communication—finding out what

Katrina Surge Line ↗
24.6 ft

This is what a typical Timber Ridge home looked like during the height of Katrina's surge. The surge was twenty-eight feet in other parts of the city. *Illustration courtesy of Wendy Roussin.*

was going on—was a critical problem in the immediate months following Katrina. Austin admitted that once his office reopened in a trailer in War Memorial Park, his role early on was less about helping people buy and sell property and more about counseling people about their options.[14]

With Fleitas Avenue just north of Second Street the home of a food tent, an adjacent athletic field was the logical location for a tent city constructed by the navy Seabees. Construction began on September 23, and families were moving into the seventy-four hard-backed tents as early as Monday, October 3. South of Second Street, War Memorial Park became the logical temporary location for a new "businesses district." A number of businesses reopened quite quickly after the storm largely in trailers and motor homes. For instance, the flooded downtown Hancock Bank was unusable to serve its customers in Pass Christian, so the bank deployed a repossessed mobile home to the park. The bank, with armed security personnel watching over it, placed folding tables outside the motor home along with an "Open for Business" sign. Hancock Bank quickly located its ATMs and secured the money that was in them. Then, the bank literally laundered the money—that is, employees washed the paper money in washing machines and then ironed the bills so the money could be used immediately. And Hancock Bank became

The U.S. Navy Seabees building cabin-like units called "strong-backed tents" as temporary emergency housing for Pass Christian residents. *Courtesy of John Fleck/FEMA, October 4, 2005.*

famous in those early days after the storm, offering $200 to any person with "credibility," requiring only that he or she sign an IOU with his or her name and address. The gesture resulted in over $3.5 million doled out (over the entire coast), with only about $200,000 never repaid. Bank president George Schloegel said, "If 99.9 percent of the public weren't honest, we couldn't run a bank. It's built on people. Regardless of the documentation on us, it's built on people doing what they say they are going to do."[15]

Before long, War Memorial Park was lined with trailers occupied by businesses; including Ellis Realty, Mississippi Coast Realty, the Peoples Bank, State Farm Insurance, Super Happy Ice (convenience store) and eventually Pirate's Cove (restaurant).

Despite the size of Pass Christian's public library, it had been cutting edge compared to others on the coast. Back in 1993, it became the first public library on the coast to have public access computers, even before Gulfport, Biloxi, Long Beach and Bay St. Louis. The distinction was achieved by being one of four rural areas in Mississippi that received a U.S. Department of Agriculture grant. Librarian Kathryn "Sally" James remembers people lining up to use the three library computers. The Pass's library, among the many victims of Katrina, eventually reopened in War Memorial Park. James managed to salvage 2,800 books out of a collection of 40,000. As the first step in rebuilding the library, James had a doublewide trailer at the park provided by Dupont DeLisle and went to work. Naperville, Illinois, became a "sister" library and funneled DVDs, CDs and VHS tapes to the Pass. The state of Texas sent 17,000 books right after the hurricane. Three Methodist Church groups from Kentucky built the shelving for books and other materials in the doublewide. Many books that could not fit in the limited space of the trailer were placed in warehouse storage while other books were part of numerous book sales that raised $10,000 for the library early on. Perhaps more importantly, the library became a communication hub for people. James grew convinced that word of mouth would not be adequate to get the city back on its feet. He started what became known as the "Bible" in an old, spiral notebook. People would sign in and list their needs, whether it was a blue tarp to stop a roof from leaking or clearing a lot so a FEMA trailer could be put on it. Then, as volunteers arrived, they would check in at the library, take a page from the "Bible" and go do the work.[16]

When Mark LaMarca Jr. and his wife, Dawn, made their way back to the Pass the day after Katrina, they faced good and bad news. The good news was that their home, located in eastern Pass Christian, had survived nicely. All the pine trees were down, and even though two had hit the roof over the garage and the roof over the porch, no water got into the home from flooding or roof damage. However, when they arrived at their restaurant on the Highway 90 beachfront between Shadowlawn and Espy Avenues, the building they had boarded up to protect was literally gone—not a trace of it. Like most of the buildings on the beachfront and downtown, only a slab remained. With the restaurant gone, the LaMarcas toughed it out at their home with no running water and electricity and then left for Destin, Florida, for a couple weeks just to get away. All the while, Dawn felt "lost" and kept asking herself, "What will we do?" When they returned, it was quickly back to business. LaMarca's brother owned Lifetime Portable Buildings in Gulfport. So, with a portable building in hand, the LaMarcas turned their "equipment guy" loose to install a twenty-four-inch grill to cook burgers and two ten-inch stone burners. After adding a three-compartment sink and getting approval by the health department, Pirate's Cove was back and open serving mostly burgers and hot dogs at War Memorial Park in November 2005.

Jennifer Hendrick and Scott Niolet spent two nights sleeping in their Cadillac Escalade with nine dogs before a third-floor room at the Red Roof Inn near Dothan, Alabama, opened up. Niolet was keeping up with

Hurricane Katrina by watching a TV installed in the Escalade. By the time he and Hendrick could make their way back to the Pass, they were expecting the worst, and their expectations were realized. The one-time Live Oak Animal Hospital was just a shell with debris piled everywhere. The few animals that had by necessity been left behind were nowhere to be found and almost certainly had perished in the twenty-eight-foot surge. Hendrick searched in the rubble and then sat on the slab in tears. Hendrick and Niolet ultimately headed north into DeLisle and slept in a tent for several nights, surviving on MREs (Meals Ready to Eat) and Skittles before going to Niolet's brother's home in Gulfport. They stayed in Gulfport until a FEMA trailer was delivered to the driveway of their uninhabitable flooded home in Timber Ridge in November 2005. Hendrick volunteered helping people with their pets, but her business was destroyed. She thought about how to bring the business back in temporary facilities in the short term while contemplating what to do in the long term.

What would be a bigger step toward "normalcy" than receiving mail? Riding out the storm six miles away in Long Beach, Postmaster Pete McGoey quickly learned how foolish it had been to simply make sure all electrical equipment was off the floor of his post office. After using a four-wheeler to traverse around seven homes that had floated and been deposited in the middle of North Street, McGoey arrived at the destroyed Pass Christian Post Office. With the logical assumption that Pass Christian would not be navigable to physically deliver the mail for months, about two weeks after the storm McGoey and his workers—with the assistance of Harrison County supervisor Marvin Ladner—set up a circus tent on a soccer field parking lot off Espy Avenue for people to come and get their mail. With mail available, if through an unconventional delivery method, again some sort of "normalcy" or routine had returned for residents. Eventually, McGoey rolled in four trailers, which became the "home" of the Pass Christian Post Office for nearly three years. In those initial five months after Katrina, though, McGoey so impressed the postal service office in Jackson with how quickly and efficiently he set up temporary post office headquarters that he was asked to write the new standard operating procedure (SOP) for the postal system—a blueprint, if you will, about how to get the mail service up and running after the destruction of a post office and surrounding city. Meanwhile, in February 2006, McGoey became the postmaster in neighboring Long Beach, where he lived.

Churches in Pass Christian did not fare well. For example, St. Paul Catholic Church on historic Scenic Drive was completely gutted by the surge.

Pass Christian U.S. Post Office destroyed by Katrina's surge. *Courtesy of Doug Kyle/U.S. Postal Service.*

St. Paul had occupied the Scenic Drive location for over 150 years. In 1969, when Hurricane Camille destroyed the church that had been erected in the 1870s and repaired after the 1915 New Orleans hurricane, a new church was built for utility; its form followed function, not architectural beauty. The A-framed steel structure opened in 1972 and stood out like a sore thumb compared to all the historic homes on Scenic Drive. But designers promised that because of its aerodynamic frame, winds—even of the magnitude of Hurricane Camille—would not blow it away. Sure enough, the structure survived Katrina's winds, but the surge destroyed everything but the frame. Amazingly, though, inside the battered church a large crucifix hanging from the ceiling on two thin wires and two stained-glass windows depicting Stations of the Cross were intact. An article in the *Tampa Tribune* on September 4 indicated that the few residents remaining in the Pass characterized the undamaged crucifix and windows as "the miracle of St. Paul's Church." The destruction of the church by Katrina caused years of controversy and lawsuits in this Catholic diocese. A fight ensued about consolidating St. Paul and Holy Family (Our Lady of Lourdes) parishes into one and relocating the main church away from St. Paul's Scenic Drive site.

There was no conflict for First Baptist Church pastor Bill Smith and his wife, Carolyn, who watched the storm from their Long Beach home, located thirty-two feet above sea level. Looking out from their boarded up home, Carolyn Smith said she was "not aware of people dying a mile away." But she and her husband found out quickly that Hurricane Katrina had been like none before it. When they arrived at First Baptist Church, near War Memorial Park, they saw a sanctuary barely standing and not salvageable. The large altar cross remained, dangling by one nail in the wreckage. The two-story education building was still standing but had eighteen inches of muck in the first floor. The children's building had been washed off its foundation and collapsed, again unsalvageable. First Baptist moved quickly because of the help of other churches around the country. The education-building roof had survived, so after gutting out the first floor, volunteers worked to close in the walls and then finished the interior drywall. By November, with running water and sewer restored, the education building was being used for services as a temporary sanctuary. By December 2005, the education building, almost miraculously, had been totally rebuilt.

Meanwhile, when Trinity Episcopal Church pastor Christopher Colby arrived at his church by foot shortly after the storm, all he saw was the roof and the floor of the main church. A metal pulpit was on the ground outside the building; the church's processional cross was found by Campus Crusade kids buried in the sand; the missile stand from the altar was found and refurbished; and of course, the altar cross he had stashed in the trunk of his car when evacuating was safe. But there were no books, artwork, furniture or musical instruments, and thirty-two twelve-foot pews were simply gone. Two of the other main buildings on the beachfront property were also missing. At first, Colby decided to hold worship services behind his garage at home, which had received water damage on the first floor but was livable. Then, the Episcopal bishop provided a tent, which was erected on the church site. Quickly, that became unacceptable to the city. Trinity was the only major building still standing on the beachfront in the western part of town, and the debris and isolated nature made it unsafe. Eventually, the First Methodist Church, which was refurbished from its water damage, became the site where Colby held worship service for the 40 percent of the congregation that remained. Besides St. Paul's, First Baptist Church's and Trinity's destruction, Our Mother of Mercy Church of the St. Joseph of the

Only the shell of Trinity Episcopal Church remained after Hurricane Katrina. *Courtesy of Mark Wolfe/FEMA, September 14, 2005.*

Sacred Heart was heavily damaged, and Goodwill Missionary Baptist Church and First Missionary Baptist Church were destroyed.

Across the street diagonally from the Trinity Episcopal Church, Father Colby observed that what once was the Pass Christian Middle School had become a pile of bricks. He was astonished because the Works Progress Administration (WPA) built the building during the Depression, and it had survived every hurricane since, including Hurricane Camille. The Pass Christian School District annually is one of the best in Mississippi. Each year when Mississippi is heralded as one of the worst states in the United States for education, be assured it is not because of the Pass Christian School District. The school district earned the highest academic performance level rating in the state—Star District. And, in 2005—before Katrina—Pass Christian High School was recognized by the U.S. Department of Education as a Blue Ribbon School of Excellence. Frankly, for a school district with nearly 70 percent of students qualifying for free or reduced-cost lunches, its sustained high academic performance is remarkable. For the 2004–05 academic year—the year before Katrina—the school district had a total of 1,980 students, with 60 percent white, 35 percent African American, 3 percent Asian and 2 percent Hispanic. So when Hurricane Katrina left the district with only one school that could be repaired and used, Superintendent Sue Matheson, business manager Marsha Garziano and the rest of the administration faced a daunting task. The middle school at the corner of Church Avenue and Second Street was destroyed; the elementary school on North Street was destroyed, and across the street the high school had received seventeen feet of water, making the first floor uninhabitable. And DeLisle Elementary north of the city had experienced some flooding. Garziano called those early days after the storm "chaotic." DeLisle Elementary is where the school district decided to start. The school had eighteen inches of water, so ServPro was brought in to make the school usable. The well-known Roy Anderson Company was hired to clear the wooded land next to DeLisle Elementary so that portable classrooms could be brought in. Garziano said the district then made an educated guess about how many trailers it would need to house all the students from the middle school through the high school and elementary students from elsewhere in the city who would not fit in the limited space of DeLisle Elementary. That guess was between forty-five and fifty trailers, including one trailer for the superintendent and associated administrators, one for maintenance and transportation and one for special education, curriculum and FEMA. While the trailers were provided through FEMA and lined up next to the elementary school, all the furnishings and supplies came from donations, big and small. Meanwhile, the one water well that served DeLisle Elementary before the storm was not enough, but after some coaxing by the district, FEMA agreed to pay for the drilling of a second well to serve all the portable classrooms. Within six weeks of the storm—on Monday, October 10, to be exact—more than two hundred elementary students and teachers from the Pass and DeLisle met for classes in the repaired building. The next day, President George W. Bush and First Lady Laura dropped in to thank educators for getting the school up and running and congratulate the district for Pass Christian High School being named a Blue Ribbon School—one of only four in the state. Pass Christian Middle School and High School students returned to classes in the modular structures on Monday, October 17, at first with about one thousand students, a little more than half as many students as before the storm. In those early months after the hurricane, all the students—not just the pre-storm 70 percent—received free meals courtesy of the government.

In the meantime, volunteers started arriving in coastal cities almost immediately, and Pass Christian was no exception. While the American Red Cross was largely absent in the Pass, the Salvation Army was present on a daily basis and the AmeriCorps of St. Louis, Missouri, became a vital part of the cleanup and eventual recovery. Civic groups and college students from

FEMA provided portable classrooms for the temporary location of Pass Christian Middle School and High School in DeLisle. *Courtesy of Mark Wolfe/FEMA, December 6, 2005.*

all over the country poured into the Pass as well, but by far, religious-affiliated groups saved the day. While FEMA created food tents and the Salvation Army provided lunch-type meals in various locations, church groups rolled in not for weeks or months but for years and years after Hurricane Katrina. And Cheeseburger Restaurants' founders Laren Gartner and Edna Bayliff formed a special bond with the Pass. They brought in a group that served some twenty thousand meals for ten days in October to residents who had lost their homes as well as volunteers. Gartner and Bayliff, on return trips to Pass Christian over the years to bring donations for police and the like, said that they felt as if they were all Pass residents. Meanwhile, many of the church-affiliated volunteers did several "tours of duty," having volunteered and then concluded that the recovery would be measured in years, not months or weeks. The main task of these volunteers was helping residents gut their homes and clean their properties in preparation for FEMA trailers and/or to rebuild. The gutting of a home consisted of tearing out all the drywall and floors—getting the home down to the two-by-four frame or studs. This allowed for the frame to dry and made the home ready to be rebuilt. It sounds like a simple enough task, but it was a nasty and sometimes dangerous job navigating the muck inside the home while ripping it down to the studs with wrecking bars and sledgehammers. It was also a tricky job because of the emotions of the owners. This was someone's home. To go in with reckless abandon and knock walls down like some of the home makeover TV shows would be disrespectful and troubling to the owners. Without the church-affiliated volunteers arriving in large numbers, Pass Christian—and the rest of the coast for that matter—would not have been able to start the recovery as quickly as it did. In a one-

FEMA operations section chief Eric Gentry (left) speaking with AmeriCorps volunteers at the tent city in Pass Christian. *Courtesy of Mark Wolfe/FEMA, February 21, 2006.*

year commemorative issue of the *Sun Herald* of Biloxi, the newspaper paid tribute to the many church and other affiliated groups that sent people to help on the coast with a twenty-five-page special section.

While volunteers helped residents ready their homes for rebuilding, people started moving into FEMA campers and trailers. When state representative Diane C. Peranich of District 121, which includes Pass Christian, and her husband first approached their DeLisle home, they noticed cushions and other items along the street that had been inside. The home itself, as Peranich described, was "horrible" and uninhabitable, destroyed by five or six feet of water. With no place to stay initially, and because her son was among the power company's essential personnel, Peranich and her husband were transported to Bay St. Louis, and for three nights, they stayed at a service center that had been set up for power company employees. Eventually, they stayed with their son, John, whose home, with the help of a generator running a pump for water and sewer service, was livable. But over the longer term, Peranich got a FEMA camper on the property of her flooded home and utilized two food tents in Pass Christian for many of her meals. As Peranich explained later, "Katrina was an equal opportunity destroyer."[17] Whether you had lived in a multimillion-dollar home on Scenic Drive or in the federally subsidized Camille Village on North Street, everyone was in

FEMA trailer among the debris on private property in Pass Christian. *Courtesy of Mark Wolfe/FEMA, December 21, 2005.*

the same line, eating the same food in the same FEMA tent. Peranich was also one of the many unlucky FEMA camper occupants adversely affected by the formaldehyde used in building its interior. Peranich's eyes were always red, and she couldn't sleep. She was saved, in a sense, by an electrical fire that deemed her camper unlivable. It was replaced with what she called an "actual" FEMA trailer where she and her husband lived for two years.

Once the people who, like Peranich, decided to stay had temporary housing, the next step was to rebuild. But in Pass Christian, no building permits were issued for two months after the storm. The city had quickly set up trailers across from War Memorial Park, and the building code and code enforcement office was open; however, permits were not being expedited. Many contractors waited and waited while individuals rebuilding for themselves got tired and started without the proper permits. Finally, on November 3, 2005, the board of aldermen replaced an individual who was in charge of issuing building permits with a team from Florida. Finally, contractors and residents could acquire building permits, allowing temporary power poles to be installed on their property by Mississippi Power, which was necessary for construction to begin.

The Pass Christian police used the Shell station as a command center for three to five weeks, until the department moved to operate out of essentially a horse trailer across from War Memorial Park. FEMA, in also occupying the Shell gas station property for the emergency rescue and recovery effort, was a benevolent dictator. While taking over Tommy Allison's C&J Quickstop, FEMA provided fuel for Allison's needs but, more importantly, allowed him to rebuild. Eleven feet of water had made its way into the Shell station during the storm, ripping it apart with only the outer walls remaining. So starting about ten days after the storm, without a building permit but with the city's knowledge, Allison picked up hourly workers congregated each day at the community center on Espy Avenue, drove to the Shell station and worked all day rebuilding his livelihood. Allison returned the workers to the community center each night. As the critical first few months passed, FEMA officials told Allison to let them know two weeks before he was ready to reopen, and their FEMA operation would vacate the premises. Some three months and $340,000 later, the C&J Quickstop reopened on December 8, 2005. Allison's business was the very first to reopen in its original location in Pass Christian. For the first time since the end of August, residents could buy gasoline and diesel fuel within the city limits.

One of the largest employers in the Pass—probably only Walmart and the Pass Christian School District employ more—was in a relatively good position after Hurricane Katrina; everyone else's bad news would be good business news for it. Gulf Coast Pre-Stress, Inc. (GCP), was established in 1967 and located in the Pass Christian Industrial Park on north Market Street. Most Pass residents knew the company by observing large flatbed diesel trucks carrying concrete pilings west on North Street to Henderson Avenue and then south to Highway 90. Some of the pilings are so large that each truck could carry only one. GCP produces not only pre-stressed concrete components for bridge, marine and structural industries but also concrete platforms for the petrochemical industry. Because GCP's products are large and difficult to deliver, the company's market is in a radius of only about 350 to 400 miles, roughly from Texas to Florida and north into Tennessee. So when Hurricane Katrina flooded GCP with fifteen feet of water, causing extensive damage to virtually all of the company's cranes, jacks and other equipment, the company had to act quickly. The Bay of St. Louis and Biloxi Bay Bridges on Highway 90 and the twin span on I-10 from Slidell to New Orleans over Lake Ponchartrain were all destroyed, so demand for GCP's products was about to hit the roof. Within a month and a half, GCP had repaired all the equipment that was repairable, replaced those pieces of equipment needed to make pre-stressed components for bridges and was back in business. Justin Yard was in Boise, Idaho, working for a lumber company when Hurricane Katrina came ashore in August. Yard is a Long Beach High School graduate who met a Biloxi girl while attending the University of Southern Mississippi in Hattiesburg and married her in March 2005. He and his wife decided that they wanted to raise a family on the coast, not in the Pacific Northwest. Yard had worked part-time as a rigger for GCP in the summers back when he was a high school student, loading barges and the like. So when he called the company seeking a job after Katrina, he quickly was hired to manage shipping. Yard, who is now vice-president of sales, arrived in November 2005, as the company was gearing up for the orders that would come out of the destruction of bridges near and far. The company's manpower expanded to 350 workers, but because of the demand associated with Hurricane Katrina, GCP bid only on those products it would be able to deliver on an accelerated construction schedule. In other words, GCP was not large enough to meet all the demand. GCP was at full capacity building and delivering piles and splice girders for the Bay of St. Louis and Biloxi Bay Bridge projects as well as the I-10 twin span in Louisiana.

During the first few months after the storm and extending into years, Robin Roberts not only provided a much-needed boost in morale by shining a national spotlight on Pass Christian's plight but also brought resources. For Roberts, Pass Christian's survival was personal. The daughter of Lawrence and Lucimarian Roberts, highly respected members of the community, Roberts was born in Alabama but raised in Pass Christian. The story is often told about Robin Roberts driving the school bus as a part-time job while going to high school. Since FEMA provided trailers for portable classrooms but no furnishings, the school district is where Roberts and *Good Morning America* started. They teamed up with Staples to provide an entire truckload of school supplies for the district. Meanwhile, when Roberts and *GMA* arrived in the Pass on September 24, 2005, Roberts couldn't help but get emotional. She came with a plan for *GMA* to partner over the next year with the Salvation Army and AmeriCorps to work hard helping with Pass Christian's overall recovery. On November 4, a joint Long Beach and Pass Christian homecoming dance was featured on *GMA*; the cities were doing everything they could be bring some "normalcy" to students' lives. On December 22, *GMA* and Roberts appeared live from the wreckage that was once St. Paul Catholic Church. This marked just the start for Robin Roberts's crusade for the city. Mayor Chipper McDermott probably best described what Roberts meant to the Pass during the critical months after Hurricane Katrina. McDermott said Roberts "meant to us what seafood means to Louisiana."

As the New Year approached, Perry Jenkins and his brothers worked diligently to rebuild Southern Printing and Silkscreening. Jenkins rode out the storm in the East End fire station as a volunteer firefighter, watching water from Katrina's surge rise four feet into the building. Even before the surge completely receded, Perry made his way downtown to check his business. He found chest-high water remaining inside his Southern Printing building, so covering the computers and large equipment with plastic had proved fruitless. In addition, his home floated off of its pilings and crashed partially into the street, a total loss. Jenkins briefly stayed at his brother's home off Demourelle Road and then lived in a tent for about six weeks until a FEMA trailer arrived. In the flooding, $300,000 worth of equipment was lost, but the brothers banded together, rebuilt the insides of the business and gradually bought equipment as they could afford it. They reopened in January 2006 despite the fact that few of their customers were back in business.

Chapter 3

GAZEBO GAZETTE

A Newspaper Is Born

It [Gazebo Gazette] was just a little survival sheet and has now evolved into a little weekly newspaper.
—*state representative Diane C. Peranich, District 121*

On January 13, 2006—about four and a half months after Hurricane Katrina—the *Gazebo Gazette* emerged in Pass Christian as an eight-page "newsletter," declaring: "Welcome to the *Gazebo Gazette*! The *Gazebo* is a place where we can meet to discuss and share resources, news and ideas." While the AmeriCorps volunteers from St. Louis, Missouri, became and remained the main news gatherers for the *Gazette* over the first six months of its existence, Evelina Shmukler became the driving force and eventually the editor in chief and publisher of the fledgling newsletter.

Shmukler arrived as a journalist to cover Hurricane Katrina for the *Wall Street Journal* just days after the storm and found the "devastation overwhelming."[18] Using the local Biloxi newspaper, the *Sun Herald*, as "base camp," Shmukler at the beginning followed the National Guard around chronicling its activities, which included distributing water and food to people who had survived and stayed. Shmukler, after staying a couple of nights on the floor of a *Sun Herald* reporter's apartment, eventually found a decent hotel to work from in Mobile, Alabama, some seventy miles due east on I-10. Shmukler traveled to the Mississippi Gulf Coast each day from Mobile and visited cities such as Pascagoula, Bay St. Louis, Waveland and the like. As the bulk of the national media focused on the ongoing catastrophe in New Orleans, Shmukler continued to

Volume 1, Issue 1 — January 13, 2006 — FREE

PASS CHRISTIAN
GAZEBO GAZETTE

A Weekly Newsletter for Residents and Friends of Pass Christian, Mississippi
Visit us online at gazebo passchristian.net

Welcome to the GAZEBO GAZETTE!

The **GAZEBO** is a place where we can meet to discuss and share resources, news and ideas

We publish weekly, on Fridays You can find issues of the **GAZEBO** online and at your local businesses, churches and city buildings. Want to distribute the **GAZEBO** at your church or business? Contact us!

We are produced entirely by volunteers, including the team from AmeriCorps St. Louis and private individuals Would you or your group like to get involved? Contact us!

Please send your news, notices, comments, questions and ideas – this is your newspaper. Email us at pcgazebo@gmail.com or call 404-275-2774.

See you next week!

In this week's issue...

City Debates Debris Clean-Up Process

➤ Discussion of the **debris clean-up** process dominated Tuesday's City Council meeting Aldermen peppered representatives of the U S Army Corps of Engineers and its contractor, Ash-Britt, with questions about both the **pace** of the clean-up effort and the lack of work being given to **local contractors.**

➤ Addressing the pace of debris clean-up, an Ash-Britt representative said that the process of gathering right-of-entry forms (ROEs), as well as the need to wait for EPA and Mississippi Department of Environmental Quality guidelines, has slowed the process down, but that they are now on the verge of getting the ball rolling

➤ He said that **the first demolition of a home took place on Monday, Jan. 9**; the goal is to demolish 40-50 homes a day, he said They have received **1,215 ROE forms,** out of a total expected 2,200 ROE forms, and have inspected 963 properties. He also said that they have completed 95% of the right-of-way removal

➤ AshBritt also said that 20 of the 21 contractors it has hired were from the state of Mississippi, but vowed to involve **more local contractors** – that is, those from the Pass Christian area and within the Pass Christian school district – in their work.

➤ The board decided to continue with the Army Corps but review the progress that has been made by the Army Corps and AshBritt in **two weeks.** The board also agreed to consider appointing an independent volunteer to monitor the debris clean-up process.

➤ The board approved the Church Street Baseball Park as a location for a trailer park. It also found out that the school district has decided not to allow trailers on a site south of the football field; the board asked for a school board representative to address the board with its concerns. FEMA is also examining the possibility of putting a trailer park on North, between Henderson and Church.

Continued on page 2

Randal Perkins, managing vice president of Ashbritt Inc , answers tough questions at the January 10 town meeting.

PHOTO BY JODI HILTON

First issue of the *Gazebo Gazette,* January 13, 2006. *Courtesy of the Gazebo Gazette.*

cover Mississippi. Exactly one week after Katrina, on September 5, Shmukler looked at a map of the coast, noticed Pass Christian at the extreme southwest corner of Harrison County and decided to explore. Once Shmukler arrived in the Pass, she observed that "the town was just flattened, like not even a ghost town, just matchsticks everywhere, and all the buildings just covered with this dust, powder, and it smelled awful, and it was just, it was terrible."[19]

Three weeks of reporting on the Mississippi Gulf Coast devastation profoundly affected Shmukler. She headed home to Atlanta for a break and her mother later noted that Shmukler did not speak for two days. Eventually, she checked in with the *Wall Street Journal* office and staff members, and after hearing the amazing stories told about the rubble that was once the coast, they urged her to return. Shmukler did not want to return; in fact, she wanted to try to forget what she had witnessed in those three weeks on the coast. However, Shmukler was persuaded to return by colleagues who tapped into her desire to help people, which was part of the reason she had become a journalist in the first place. But with New Orleans still the major story nationwide, Shmukler's stories filed after her return about the devastation in Mississippi rarely made it to the print version of the *Wall Street Journal*, with most being posted only online. Shmukler hated reporting on Katrina's aftermath, but she got a keen sense of satisfaction whenever she could help residents by sharing water or providing gasoline to those who needed it. Once back in Atlanta again, Shmukler continued to be frustrated because *the* story was New Orleans, and seemingly none of her stories about Pass Christian and other Mississippi coast cities were going to see the light of day. It became glaringly apparent that she was no longer needed by the *Wall Street Journal*. She contemplated quitting journalism and perhaps going back to graduate school. But in October, Shmukler decided to return to the coast—this time as a volunteer not a journalist.

Pass Christian alderman Joseph Piernas Sr., with whom Shmukler had stayed in contact as a reporter, told her that with winter approaching, the biggest need for those staying in the city was sleeping bags and tents. There did not seem to be any other good alternatives to house residents and volunteers over the winter. So Shmukler sent out e-mails to former colleagues, friends and relatives explaining the need. Money started flowing in, enough that she was able to buy sixty sleeping bags and five tents, receiving a small discount from the Coleman outlet store in Atlanta. Shmukler, her sister and her sister's boyfriend (now husband) traveled to Pass Christian over the Thanksgiving holiday, distributed the sleeping bags and tents and then volunteered at one of the many points of distribution, or PODs. During the time, Shmukler stayed nights with the fire department on a cot. Back and forth, Shmukler went from her home in Atlanta to Mississippi and then back again.

Shmukler returned to Pass Christian the day after Christmas with a group of friends. While volunteering, which included cleaning up lots and helping set up another POD that authorities were moving, Shmukler and friends stayed in a mobile home donated to the city library that was not yet filled with books. She stayed there courtesy of the local librarian, Kathryn "Sally" James. It was at this point that James mentioned to Shmukler that the lack of communication within the community was hampering volunteers' efforts and the coordination of the city's rebuilding. The library had become a sort of central meeting place and clearinghouse for information largely because of James. Up until this point, AmeriCorps volunteers had periodically distributed a one- or two-page "newsletter" with essentially a bulleted list of news items and a phone list on the back. A more consistent information pipeline was clearly needed, and after brainstorming, it was decided that AmeriCorps volunteers would gather information and feed it to Shmukler, who would be back in Atlanta. She would then edit the materials; make multiple copies and overnight the "newsletter" via FedEx back to the Pass for distribution.

Being a veteran journalist, Shmukler wanted a formal name for the publication. How the "newsletter" became the *Gazebo Gazette* was the result of Shmukler's background and community input, a two-pronged formula that became the blueprint for the publication's evolution. Initially, Shmukler thought the name the *Pass Christian Gazette* would work nicely. Shmukler favored "gazette" over "tribune," "times," "herald" and other names for two reasons: first, many of the names used for newspapers seemed generic to Shmukler, so she preferred the less common "gazette." Second, "gazette" sounds like the Russian word for newspaper, *gazeta*, and since Shmukler was born in the Ukraine when it was part of the Soviet Union, this would clearly place her stamp on the publication. Shmukler shared her proposed name via e-mail with alderman Piernas, who, along with Sally James, was among a core group of residents pushing for a more consistent newsletter in the city. In a January 6, 2006 e-mail, Shmukler sent Piernas a prototype of what was labeled the *Pass Christian Gazette*. Piernas thought the prototype looked great but suggested that perhaps the *Pass Christian Gazebo* would be better than "gazette" because the gazebo in War Memorial Park was a symbol of the city and appeared on business cards, stationery and the like. The solution seemed simple to Shmukler: *Gazebo Gazette* would appear in large bold print on the front page nameplate and above it in smaller bold letters "Pass Christian" would be written. At the bottom of the nameplate in smaller, less obtrusive print, Shmukler explained succinctly what this

The new gazebo in War Memorial Park.

fledgling publication was all about: "A Weekly Newsletter for Residents and Friends of Pass Christian, Mississippi."[20]

The *Gazette*'s Volume 1, Issue 1 front page sadly reflected perfectly Pass Christian's stage of recovery four and half months after Katrina. While some individuals had started to rebuild their homes and War Memorial Park hosted businesses that had reopened in temporary quarters, debris cleanup remained front and center. The Army Corps of Engineers contracted with Ash-Britt, Inc., to remove the tons of debris that was once homes and businesses. Once the cleanup was well underway, the concerns related to the pace of the debris removal and the lack of work being subcontracted out to local haulers. And while the general cleanup of the streets and public property was one issue, demolishing and removing condemned homes on private property was quite another.[21] In fact, the first razing of the remains of a home on private property—which didn't happen until right of way entry forms (ROEs) were obtained and Environmental Protection Agency and Mississippi Department of Environmental Quality guidelines were followed—occurred on January 9, 2006, 132 days after Hurricane Katrina. The article about the debris cleanup progress accompanied by a photograph of Ash-Britt managing vice-president Randal Perkins was the only story on the front page. The only other major story in the very first *Gazette* was about the St. Paul Carnival Association's seventy-sixth-annual Mardi Gras celebration, scheduled for February 26. Perhaps more importantly, though, the *Gazette* listed every business open in the Pass five months after the storm—a number you could count on the fingers of two hands. Hancock Bank, the Peoples Bank, State Farm Insurance, Mississippi Coast Realty, Ellis Realty Group, Super Happy Ice Cream Convenience Store and Pirate's Cove Sandwich Shop, along with the Shell station at the corner of Henderson Avenue and North Street, were the only businesses in Pass Christian.

By the publishing of the *Gazette*'s third issue, a major shake up of the board of aldermen was beginning. The front-page story said that Ward 4 alderman Donald Moore, who lived in the middle-class neighborhood of Timber Ridge, was resigning. Moore explained that he was not rebuilding his destroyed Timber Ridge home; instead, he was building a new home outside Ward 4. So, since he would be required to resign when he officially moved into his new home and he wanted to spend more time with his wife and young children, as well as give proper attention to his busy law practice, he decided to resign immediately. Privately, Moore lamented that not one home in Timber Ridge was livable. Every home either sustained so much flood damage that it would have to be totally gutted and rebuilt top to bottom, or it had been lifted off its pilings or foundation and existed only as a pile of rubble. Moore was a realist; it was going to be between five and ten years before Timber Ridge would be anywhere near back to "normal," and if he stayed, his children's formative years would be difficult among the demolition and rebuilding in the neighborhood. Eventually, the city council set March 23 as a date for a special election to fill the unexpired term of Donald Moore.

Meanwhile, for the first six issues, each *Gazette* was eight pages, copied front and back onto standard eight-and-a-half- by eleven-inch paper and distributed

Pass Christian homes on the Bay of St. Louis. All received both surge and wind damage. *Courtesy of Huey Bang.*

for free at the Pass Christian Library and city hall (both located in mobile homes near War Memorial Park), the AmeriCorps Tent, the FEMA Food Tent and the Shell station on North Street. From the very first issue, the *Gazette* was available online through the city's unofficial historian, Dan Ellis. Ellis relocated but agreed to upload the paper each week to serve those residents who had not been able to return yet. But make no mistake about it; with no power or landline telephone service in much of the city, the traditional hard copy was vitally important in keeping a weary citizenry dutifully informed.

Shmukler, you remember, was back in Atlanta creating the newspaper from information fed to her from AmeriCorps volunteers. All the while, Shmukler faced an uncertain future. She applied to graduate schools with an eye toward a PhD in English. At one point, through connections her sister had, she was hired by an educational firm to travel to Abu Dhabi for one week to write a grant proposal. Shmukler contacted Sally James to inform her that the *Gazette* would have to take a week off because she had this job in Abu Dhabi. James would have none of that, arguing that people were expecting the *Gazette* and that if it disappeared for a week people would think it was gone. So that issue in the early spring of 2006 was compiled and edited in Abu Dhabi, printed in Shmukler's mom's office in Atlanta and FedExed by a friend to Pass Christian.

In the February 10, 2006 issue, the *Gazette* announced that it would accept what it termed "sponsorships" for the Mardi Gras edition of February 24 and that it would be printed using a commercial copier by Southern Printing and Silkscreening—a well-known local printer—as opposed to on an office-quality copier. This marked the first big step in the evolution of the *Gazette* into a more sophisticated "newsletter" created by volunteers. That issue was twelve pages, and it contained ads for the first time—all display ads on pages six and seven. Between 600 and 650 copies were printed and distributed in the community. From this time on, ads would become a part of the lifeblood of the *Gazette*. Some of those "sponsorships" were acquired with the help of Mayor Chipper McDermott, who, at the time, was an alderman. McDermott recalls asking Shmukler how much it cost to put the newsletter out each week. He recalled ninety dollars a week as the figure thrown out. Understanding the importance the newsletter was to the survival of the city, McDermott talked with businesses about buying fifteen- and twenty-five-dollar ads to, at the very least, cover Shmukler's costs.

The March 17 issue expanded to sixteen pages to accommodate the ads for Ward 4 aldermen candidates and thus give adequate "voice" to the candidates prior to the special election filling the unexpired term of Donald Moore. The paper returned to twelve pages the following week and fluctuated between twelve and sixteen pages for the next nine issues. The March 24 issue marked the beginning of "opinion" pieces appearing in the *Gazette*, with a letter from a prominent resident explaining what he had learned from the volumes of volunteers who had helped clean up Pass Christian in the months since Katrina.

The first controversy regarding the *Gazette* was revealed in the April 21 issue. A group called the Community Outreach Network had been listed among the volunteer organizations helping with the publishing of the paper. A news story reported that Community Outreach Network director James Garrett Jr. was arrested for one count of prescription forgery and one count of being a fugitive from a probation warrant out of Texas. The article said that the Community Outreach Network "was instrumental in organizing the computer and office lab in War Memorial Park and bringing volunteers to the city to do repair and cleanup activities, as well as obtaining donated goods and services for citizens." *Gazette* editor in chief Evelina Shmukler added an "editor's note" to the story. Shmukler stated that she hoped that the news would "not overshadow the good work he has done here in the

Pass, nor that done by countless other volunteers who have come here." And Shmukler reminded readers that "everyone is innocent until proven otherwise."[22] Nevertheless, after four weeks of thanking the Community Outreach Network for its assistance in putting together the *Gazette*, the organization was dropped from the *Gazette*'s "thank-you" list the very next issue and was never again acknowledged in the newspaper.

As the "newsletter" evolved, so, too, did Shmukler's thinking and ultimately her entire life. First, she had the desire to add more pages to include more news, but using a standard copier to print was much more expensive than standard newsprint. In fact, Shmukler figured that it would be less expensive to print 3,000 copies on newsprint than it cost to produce 650 on a commercial copier. So newsprint was the route to go. After finding out the closest community newspaper to Pass Christian—the *Sea Coast Echo* of Bay St. Louis—had lost its printing presses in Hurricane Katrina and was using the *Picayune Item*'s, she contacted the *Picayune* newspaper owners, and they offered to print the *Gazebo* at a "great price." Next, if Shmukler were to expand coverage, more revenue would be needed. She toyed with the options of either staying a nonprofit and writing grants to keep the publication going—which included paperwork and a headache she was not looking forward to—or running the newspaper as a business. So as her twenty-ninth birthday neared, Shmukler made a dramatic, life-changing decision. The newspaper was becoming "professional," and there would be no way that Shmukler could serve as editor and publisher from Atlanta. So in May 2006, in time to see the very first true "newspaper" *Gazebo Gazette* hit the streets, Shmukler moved from Atlanta to the Mississippi Gulf Coast. She decided she would sustain herself by grant writing for area organizations and freelance writing while running the newspaper and see where the "business" stood in one year. Shmukler seemingly had a perfect attitude starting a new business where there were no guarantees. She thought that if the newspaper survived and flourished, great. But if it did not, it would be something she did in her twenties that was fun and beneficial.

The May 26, 2006 issue heralded the *Gazette*'s growing from a "newsletter" to a newspaper. In fact, the banner read "A Weekly Newspaper for Residents and Friends of Pass Christian, Mississippi" rather than "Newsletter." This "new" issue was tabloid in size, printed at the *Picayune Item* and contained twenty pages of news and free community information. Three thousand copies were printed. The *Gazebo Gazette* had grown from a Xerox-copied newsletter to a full-fledged community newspaper in just under five months. A letter published from Chuck Linkey of Pass Christian describing two

PASS CHRISTIAN
GAZEBO 🕍 GAZETTE
A Newspaper for Residents and Friends of Pass Christian, Mississippi
Visit us online at www.gazebogazette.com

The *Gazebo Gazette*'s logo/nameplate. *Courtesy of the Gazebo Gazette.*

factions existing in the city—one supporting "new business, new housing, and an expanded tax base" and another seemingly "more concerned with retaining their power by keeping the tax base small"—prompted a series of letters in the coming issues about the future of the Pass. The give and take amounted to a kind of town hall discussion via the print media. Meanwhile, Linkey had gained a small amount of fame earlier in the year. Biloxi's TV station, WLOX, reported on January 17 that Linkey and his wife, Joyce, had been issued the first certificate of occupancy in Pass Christian since the hurricane. The couple was about to move into their Lemoyne Road home when Katrina's storm surge hit. Linkey had an advantage over most in rebuilding. He was a contractor who wisely had moved all his tools out of harm's way, which allowed him to rebuild his home quickly.

As the newspaper was now starting to mature, changes still came about—just not as dramatic as those that had been experienced over the first twenty issues. Issue 22 on June 9, 2006, announced it would begin home delivery the following week at thirty dollars per year as opposed to forty-eight dollars per year for mailed subscriptions. Further, by Issue 24, the *Gazette* had expanded its circulation to an area north known as Diamondhead—which at that time was an unincorporated community where many residents of the Pass had moved either temporarily or permanently after Katrina.

The *Gazette* took another major step in its evolution on August 4 with its first editorial. In "It's Time for our City Council to Raise Elevations," Shmukler argued that delaying the setting of new flood elevations to allow people to rebuild at the old pre-Katrina elevations actually was stunting the rebuilding in the Pass. Increasing Cost of Compliance (ICC) funding—up to $30,000 for homeowners raising their property to new flood elevation levels—would not be granted by the federal government until the city complied with the new FEMA "guidelines" and homeowners built at those new elevated levels. Shmukler wrote: "The City Council should set a date in the future—say, 30 days from now—and raise elevations from that date forward." The paper's second editorial, "The City Council Needs to Make

Some Hard Decisions, and It Needs to Make Them Now," just two weeks later in the August 18 issue touched on the elevation topic and another controversial subject: building heights in downtown Pass Christian and along historic Scenic Drive. The editorial called for raising the current flood elevations "three feet across the board" and, at the same time, called for opposing sides to come together for a compromise about a proposed one-story height limit placed on buildings located on land between Scenic Drive and Highway 90. Shmukler wrote that the one-story limit would "strip that very expensive land of any real value." During the first week of September 2006, the city council—with the help of the mayor, who broke a tie vote—raised the building elevations by three feet in Zone A, effective October 15, perhaps the first evidence of the newspaper's influence on city policy. This opened the door for residents who had flood insurance on property that was 50 percent or more damaged to be eligible for the ICC funding. At the time, officials estimated that between two and three hundred property owners were waiting to begin rebuilding until the new flood elevations were adopted.

The August 25, 2006 Issue 32 front-page story in the commemorative edition was titled "Aug. 29, 2005: One Year Later," and it contained the names of twenty-four Pass Christian citizens who died in Hurricane Katrina.[23] The issue also included a compilation of stories that appeared in the old *Tarpon-Beacon* one year after the historic Hurricane Camille destroyed the Pass in 1969.

Later in the fall of 2006, further evidence surfaced that the newspaper was having an effect on city policy. For instance, in the October 6, 2006 issue, a "Letter to the Editor" from resident Ben C. Toledano (an attorney) expressed concern that Hancock Bank, the Peoples Bank, Mississippi Coast Realty, State Farm Insurance and other private businesses were operating on land at War Memorial Park (in temporary trailers) rent free. Toledano explained that allowing rent-free space immediately after the storm was one thing, but thirteen months had now passed since Katrina. He asked, "When was the emergency supposed to end?" About one month later, the city council passed a resolution setting rent rates for businesses operating on War Memorial Park land.

Finally, in December, the *Gazebo Gazette* took a final step toward becoming a full-fledged professional community newspaper. Shmukler opened up a business office for the paper in the post-Katrina renovated Colonnade Office Building on Second Street in downtown Pass Christian.

The *Gazebo Gazette*'s creation in January 2006 was critical to residents' being able to make informed and educated decisions about what to do with their lives. And for those who decided to stay in Pass Christian, the *Gazette* made the day-to-day drudgery of living just a little bit easier. It is not that the region's daily paper—the *Sun Herald* of Biloxi—didn't do an excellent job reporting about Hurricane Katrina and its aftermath because, in fact, the *Sun Herald* won a Pulitzer Prize for Public Service in 2006 for "providing a lifeline for devastated readers." The *Sun Herald* did its fair share of stories about Pass Christian, but it primarily had to focus on the two most populated cities, Gulfport and Biloxi. The *Gazette*, because it was targeting only Pass Christian, could give up-to-date information about businesses reopening, include all action from each board of aldermen meeting, list services, keep up with the food tent and housing situation and include minute details vital to each resident that the *Sun Herald* could not publish as a regional paper. Remarkably, the *Gazette*'s purpose matched closely to the so-called *Frontier Press* that sprang up in the United States as people moved West in the mid-1800s. The *Frontier Press*'s characteristics are strikingly similar to the *Gazette*'s, including a newspaper that maintains "continuity between old lives and new," confirms word-of-mouth communications, promotes the community "with a view to growth and prosperity," (boosterism) and gives "businesses a means to reach customers through advertising."[24] The city of Pass Christian essentially was starting over. Virtually no building in the downtown was usable, and the *Gazette* filled the city's needs very similarly to how newspapers did for new cities forming in the West 150 years earlier.

Chapter 4

PROGRESS?
THE BEST LAID PLANS...

Of all the words of mice and men, the saddest are "It might have been."
—Cat's Cradle, *Kurt Vonnegut*

Looking back years after the storm, Mayor Chipper McDermott said that the first year after Hurricane Katrina was about survival and cleaning the debris out of the city, the second year was about chasing grants of all kinds to help rebuild the city's infrastructure and the third year—2008—was the bricks-and-mortar year when many major construction projects started. All during the recovery process, exciting proposals surfaced. But throughout the recovery of Pass Christian, and particularly in the few years after the first anniversary of Hurricane Katrina, project proposals and ideas were explored that for various reasons fell by the wayside.

When the strip mall anchored by the Winn-Dixie and Rite Aid Pharmacy vanished in Hurricane Katrina's surge, it ended any hope of a grocery store returning to the Pass (the Winn-Dixie had already closed before the storm). But this was a historic and legendary site. In 1969, so the story has been repeated over the years, the Richelieu Manor Apartments stood on the property, and Hurricane Camille swept over the coast, killing twenty-three people who reportedly were partying in the apartments. The claim about an irresponsible hurricane party causing nearly two dozen deaths has been largely discredited over the years. The known facts suggest that maybe eight people in the apartments died and that there was no party. In any event, the nearly seven acres of prime commercial property between Henderson and Clarence Avenues bordering Highway 90 to the south remained empty after

Hurricane Katrina. But in September 2006, Cress Development presented preliminary plans to the Planning Commission for a two-hundred-unit condominium complex. The plans called for heights of five stories and parking underneath. The September 8 *Gazebo Gazette* front-page story indicated that the Planning Commission gave Cress Development approval to create detailed engineering plans, but the developer needed to sell 75 to 80 percent of the units to get financing. There were also worries about problems getting insurance. The condo development never got past the preliminary stages. Then, the land became embroiled in a controversy many years later when the Mississippi Department of Marine Resources' statewide land purchases were investigated. The DMR bought the beachfront property that was appraised for $5.25 million from a private citizen for $3.00 million in 2008, though the county tax roll appraisal was just $595,000. The DMR justified the purchase, which was made with a federal grant, in part because the land was high risk for future flooding and could be used for conservation efforts and public use. The DMR approached the City of Pass Christian about a partnership: the DMR would convert the land into a playground, walking trails and a dog park, and the city would maintain the property. To date, no agreement has been reached, and Mayor Chipper McDermott laments the loss of $12,000 on the tax rolls with the property transferred from private ownership to the government.

In a late November 2006 board of aldermen meeting, Mayor McDermott expressed optimism that the city could break ground on a new city hall building within six months. Further, a design by architect Larry Jaubert represented a vision of what the new structure might look like. The Jaubert design—published in the December 1 issue of the *Gazette*—was a two-story, nine-thousand-square-foot building that was inspired by the 1927 Pass Christian City Hall that had been built while McDermott's grandfather J.H. Spence was mayor. The reality was that the new city hall ended up being two one-story buildings instead, adding up to about ten thousand square feet. The city didn't break ground until April 30, 2009, two years after the mayor had hoped.

After months of consternation, the Bentonville, Arkansas–based Walmart announced in October 2006 that it would return to the Pass, but when and where was left up in the air. This fueled speculation that had started as early as November 2005, when Laura Hall, a member of Haley Barbour's redevelopment design team, revealed that Walmart had agreed to meet with her group. Hall was enthusiastic about the possibility of a new kind of Walmart returning, one that would include residential units and maybe even other stores surrounding it in the downtown. Hall went so far as to say the unique nature of their vision of Walmart might be the wave of the future. But when Walmart finalized the purchase of land bordering on the north of its old destroyed store in early 2007, the retailer announced that it would build on the same basic footprint, just a little farther back from Highway 90. Still, Walmart contended that the new building would be unique to the town and region, leaving on the table the possibility for a mixed-use development—that is, Walmart at the center of a larger residential and commercial planned community. One year later, in February 2008, Mayor Chipper McDermott declared a "touchdown" when Walmart committed to rebuild, shooting for an August 2009 opening. But none of the plans for mixed-use was even addressed; Walmart committed to and built a 150,000-square-foot store, slightly smaller than the previous and not unique in any way. Further, at the same time that the governor's redevelopment design team talked about a "new" Walmart, it also talked about a public transportation system in the city with apartments and condominiums lining the CSX railroad tracks, which the design team said would be more useful if used for commuter trains. Years later, there is no public transportation system and no housing lining the railroad tracks, and they are still used exclusively by freight trains.

One of the biggest fears for some of Pass Christian's old guard was that developers would descend on the city and line the Highway 90 beachfront with Florida panhandle–type condominiums. While the fear was palpable, there were very few "real" proposals for condos. In March 2007, MSGC Investments announced that it was bringing a $40 million condo project designed for permanent residents, not as rentals for investors. The project was named "Somerset Pass," and according to a release from the company published in the March 23, 2007 *Gazebo Gazette*, it involved thirty-six luxury 2,500-square-foot and larger units priced at between $1.1 and $1.6 million. The units were to be located in a 70-foot-tall, six-story building on Highway 90. Construction was scheduled to begin in the fall of 2007, once at least thirty reservations had been secured. The luxury condo project proposal was never mentioned again, and its SomersetPass.com website soon was abandoned.

In Mayor Chipper McDermott's State of the City address in February 2007, he talked about the city expanding to the north in the Pineville area. McDermott reasoned that the city was about to provide water and sewer service to the area anyway under a state grant, and the residents' main benefit would be lower insurance costs. Five years after the mayor broached the subject of annexation, in April 2012, Chancellor Hollis McGehee heard Pass Christian's arguments to annex about 250 to 300 homes. The city contended that residents' fire rating in the annexation area would be reduced from 8 to 6 instantly and that the city was already providing some services to the homes located in the proposed annexation area. In early May 2012, the city received word that McGehee would deny the city's request to annex 5.4 square miles in Harrison County, saying the request was not reasonable. Pass Christian city fathers initially indicated that they would appeal to the Mississippi Supreme Court, and the city filed papers to do so. But with a minimum cost of $60,000 to appeal added to the half million dollars already spent, aldermen voted three to two to withdraw the city's annexation appeal. In an editorial in the May 25, 2012 *Gazebo Gazette* titled "Fight for Annexation Was Right," Evelina Shmukler wrote that it would have been hard for a judge from the north to understand Pass Christian's "desperate need to expand its borders" given the "beating our ad valorem tax base—the city's lifeblood—took in a single day." She wrote that the judge "ignored that history, and also the future."[25] Years later, Shmukler said that most of the time she worked very hard to stay neutral on issues, but the rejection of the Pass's annexation proposal was unjust and unfair. Of little consolation was that back in November 2007, the aldermen voted to annex the forty-eight-unit Pass Marianne Condominiums southwest of the city on Highway 90 and were successful with no opposition from residents.

In September 2007, the Army Corps of Engineers raised the possibility of building a coast-long levee along the railroad tracks from the Bay of St. Louis all the way across the Mississippi coast to the Biloxi Bay, cutting through several cities, including Pass Christian. Representing the corps, Dr. Susan Rees said the railroad levee would be no higher than the current tracks in some places, but in other areas, it might raise the current tracks two or three feet. The corps' proposal, which was in a list of more than 250 possible options, including a controversial voluntary buy-out for landowners with low-lying, at-risk property, was talked about at a public hearing in the Pass. Those who opposed the levees and buy-outs argued that just talking about the proposals would scare away potential investors from the region and drive down property values. The creation of a coast-wide levee never got past the talking stages.

Perhaps the highest hopes were attached to the Harbor Town at the Pass development, which broke ground on April 16, 2008. Located on Scenic Drive just west of Market Street and stretching all the way back to Second Street, the development was to be mixed use with seventy-eight residential units and twenty-one thousand square feet of new commercial space. Harbor Town, whose slogan was "When the Future Meets the Pass," was to be four stories, and developers talked about luring in a specialty grocery store, a health spa and fitness center, a liquor store, a local restaurant, an antiques dealer and an artist. But as construction commenced and some pilings that would serve as the base of the project were built, the economy in late 2008 caused some banks to pull their financing, and by April 2009, developers faced foreclosure proceedings on part of the land. Construction stopped, and soon after, the abandoned property became an unkept blight on prime downtown Pass Christian property. The death of Harbor Town also marked the death—for the moment—of Pirate's Cove's rebuilding plan. Pirate's Cove, with its unique po' boys recipe, was the "local" restaurant that was to be part of Harbor Town. After being in War Memorial Park for over a year and a half, the LaMarcas moved their "shed turned into restaurant" to Market Street and built a small addition. The plan was clear: open the restaurant and serve the Harbor Town construction workers and then occupy a new restaurant as part of Harbor Town at the corner of Second and Market Streets. With the demise of Harbor Town, the LaMarcas now had to think about plan B, except plan B did not exist yet. Meanwhile, the abandoned Harbor Town site is now being talked about as a possible location for a new Hampton Inn.

A couple other proposed developments just outside the city limits that would have had a positive impact on Pass Christian's economy never materialized. For nearly fifty years, the Gulfshore Baptist Assembly occupied about 34 acres at historic Henderson Point in Harrison County that borders on the Pass. Before the Baptist Assembly bought the land in a federal government auction the 1950s, it had been the site of a resort during the turn of the twentieth century and was the U.S. Merchant Marine Academy in the World War II era. Hurricane Katrina destroyed every structure of the Baptist Assembly, leaving only the frame of the main building. Once a decision was made not to rebuild, the assembly decided to sell the property to developer Douglas Johnson and NewTrac East, LLC, for $18 million in December 2007. Johnson proposed a multi-use, multimillion-dollar project that he called "Gulfshore Point." His agreement with the Mississippi Baptist Convention Board (MBCB) included a promise not to build a casino and to keep the land use within the historical nature of the community. However, according to MBCB, early in 2009, Johnson withdrew his offer after the Harrison County Planning Commission twice delayed votes on regulations that affected the development.[26] Meanwhile, a second development, slated to be built on 438 acres just north of Pass Christian's city limits in Harrison County, was announced in September 2008 by Southern Gaming Thrills, LLC. Located between Bayou Portage and Wolf River Bridges, west of Discovery Bay, the proposed Blue Water Bay Resort and Casino received site approval from the Mississippi Gaming Commission. The plans called for the initial 100,000-square-foot casino with an adjoining five-hundred-room hotel to be built in the first phase, costing about $400 million and creating about 1,400 jobs. The company promised the scenic property would include preservation parks accessible by the public and managed by an unnamed conservation group. The September 26 *Gazette* carried a front-page story that included an artist's rendition of what the development would look like that jumped to pages two and three, where additional multiple drawings of this ambitious development proposal appeared. However, the project never materialized.

Chapter 5

RECOVERY

Benchmarks

Welcome back, WALMART
—Gazebo Gazette, *front-page headline, October 14, 2009*

Once Pass Christian's citizens gathered themselves from the shock of what Hurricane Katrina did to their city, the quest for normalcy began. Anything that reminded a person of his or her former life was cherished. Since trick-or-treating was an impossibility, on October 29, 2005, the city, Walmart, *Good Morning America* and Sun Audio Rentals teamed up to host a Halloween party in War Memorial Park. About one thousand kids showed up. In December 2005, a group of hardy souls organized "Christmas in the Pass" and decorated War Memorial Park, which had become the "hub" for business and government. The annual one-night event originally was designed by merchants to bring people downtown. After Katrina, it was held simply to lift spirits. However, the first major event held after the storm was the city's Mardi Gras parade, which is sponsored by the St. Paul Carnival Association. The Pass Parade dates back to the early 1900s, and according to a local historian, the late Billy Bourdin, had been cancelled only during World War II and one year during the Korean War. It is annually one of the largest parades on the Mississippi Gulf Coast. For instance, in 2005, estimates of between sixty and eighty thousand people had attended in a city whose population was fewer than seven thousand. Needless to say that even during a "normal" year in the Pass, such a crowd demanded that additional fire and police personnel be hired to keep the peace and handle emergencies, prompting police chief John Dubuisson to reveal that the best part of the celebration for him was "When it's all over, if it turns out to be a safe one."[27] In 2006, having a parade was important, even though the bulk of the people who lost their homes were either in FEMA trailers or living elsewhere. Pass Christian decided that the parade could go on, but the route was restricted to Highway 90 between Seal and Henderson Avenues instead of portions winding downtown, and the number of floats was limited to twenty-eight. *GMA*'s Robin Roberts, who continued to bring the spotlight on the plight of the city where she grew up to the rest of the country, served as the grand marshal. Roberts remembered how, as a kid, she had loved seeing parked cars all the way down Second Street to her parents' home on Oak Park Drive. At noon on February 26, 2006, citizens enjoyed normalcy for a few hours as the seventy-sixth annual Pass Parade rolled. But this was a "new" normal; at most, about ten thousand people lined Highway 90 for the scaled-down event.

Even though the Pass Parade was held five months after Katrina, some residents still lived in the FEMA tent city on Fleitas—known as the Village—and the Army Corps of Engineers' difficult job of debris removal was far from over. The tent city and the adjacent food tent were costing the government about $23,000 a day to provide essentially room and board for three hundred Pass residents left homeless by Hurricane Katrina. By March 2006, eligible residents had either been relocated to FEMA trailers or had made other housing arrangements; so FEMA closed the Village for its original purpose on March 15, 2006, six and a half months after Katrina. The tent city immediately transitioned into volunteer housing, with AmeriCorps coordinating its occupancy as college students and others descended into the city on short-term "shifts." Debris removal by the Army Corps of Engineers was originally supposed to be completed on May 31. Then it was estimated for June 30, and finally, one year after the storm, it was completed on August 28, 2006. Debris removal at times hindered the efforts to bring water and sewer service to the entire city. Hydrants were sometimes inadvertently damaged, and the large mounds of debris often were in the way of repairing and running new pipes. By early 2006, essentially all parts of the city had water and sewer service, but it was only the beginning of rebuilding the entire system permanently. Bruce Anthony of WPSCO said the city was broken down into five distinct areas, basically from east to west, and in each area new pipe was laid as needed. One of the quirks associated with FEMA funding reared its head during the rebuilding of the water and sewer system. Essentially, all new pipe installed south of the railroad tracks was covered by FEMA, while most of the pipe run north of the tracks was not. Completion of the rebuilding did not occur until 2013.

Mayor Chipper McDermott (left) with FEMA's Jody Correro outside a trailer that served as the temporary Pass Christian City Hall. *Courtesy of Mark Wolfe/FEMA, August 16, 2006.*

Immediately after the storm, Mayor Billy McDonald was either out of town or simply not able to perform the duties necessary to bring Pass Christian back. City attorney Malcolm Jones was named chief administrative assistant and basically ran the city for the next year. Alderman Donald Moore resigned early in 2006, in part because it was clear that the neighborhood he lived in and represented, Timber Ridge, was years and years away from becoming a decent place to raise his children. Huey Bang was elected to replace Moore. Eventually bowing to public pressure, McDonald resigned in the summer of 2006, and alderman-at-large Chipper McDermott ran and won the right to succeed McDonald.

Then in a special election, Philip Wittman defeated former alderman Michael Antoine to fill the vacant alderman-at-large position in early September 2006, beginning a period of stabilization for the city government. The board of aldermen was then made up of Wittman, Bang, Lou Rizzardi, Anthony Hall and Joe Piernas Sr. This board, with McDermott as mayor, stayed the same for nearly three years—until June 2, 2009, when Wittman was defeated and Rizzardi decided not to seek reelection. In those three years an unbelievable number of major decisions were made that shaped the way Pass Christian is today.

The destroyed Bay of St. Louis Bridge—which linked southwest Harrison County and Pass Christian to southeast Hancock County and Bay St. Louis—left the Pass cut off from the world to the west. For instance, with the bridge out, students from the Pass attending Catholic school in Bay St. Louis—either at St. Stanislaus or Holy Trinity—had a fifty-mile round-trip drive each day, traveling the back roads north of Pass Christian, into Hancock County and then south to one of the two schools, each located close to the beach. The Mississippi Department of Transportation (MDOT) went into action quickly to get the Bay Bridge rebuilt. First, MDOT decided that the new bridge needed to be built on a slightly different footprint to ameliorate a sharp corner that had existed as the old bridge wound into Harrison County at Henderson Point. That meant acquiring land owned by individuals, either by making an offer that was acceptable or by eminent domain. The main piece of property affected by the change in footprint was a triangular-shaped piece of land about one acre in size owned by Penny Rodrique of Pass Christian.[28] One month and one day after Hurricane Katrina—October 30, 2005—MDOT officials called Rodrique and told her they wanted to buy her land. Rodrique had operated Mississippi Coast Fireworks on the property for about twenty-five years, at first by renting the property and selling from a stand, then a tent, and finally purchasing the land and erecting a four-thousand-square-foot metal building for her retail business. MDOT offered Rodrique $416,700 as "just compensation" for property she believed was worth between $1 and $1.5 million. Publically, MDOT indicated that it was negotiating with Rodrique to buy the land, but behind the scenes, back on October 27, MDOT had filed court papers for a quick-take eminent domain action. That essentially gave the deed of Rodrique's property immediately to MDOT, and MDOT delivered the $416,700 to the court to be dispersed to Rodrique. To say Rodrique was distraught is a gross understatement. This property, in the years after her divorce, had provided a livelihood that paid for her daughter to attend top-notch private elementary and high schools and for Rodrique to go back to school for her BA at the University of Southern Mississippi. To Rodrique, MDOT was not just taking land—it was also taking a part of her past and future. Eminent domain law allowed Rodrique to reject the MDOT offer and go to court to have a jury decide "just compensation," but she no longer owned the property.

Meanwhile, the quick-take proceeding allowed MDOT to expedite rebuilding the Bay Bridge, but Granite Construction Company, in a joint venture with Archer Western Contractors, was not hired until January 2006 and did not begin work until April 2006. Granite–Archer Western—as it came to be known—had signed a rare design-build contract rather than putting the design up for bid for an architectural engineering firm to draw plans and then taking those plans and putting those out to bid for construction companies. The price tag was about $260 million for a 2.1-mile, four-lane, eighty-five-foot-high bridge with a pedestrian walkway and large shoulder lanes. Twenty months after Hurricane Katrina—in May 2007—one lane going east and one lane going west opened. And eight months after that—in January 2008—all four lanes were opened and the Bay Bridge was finished. In a *Gazebo Gazette* editorial, Evelina Shmukler applauded MDOT for "doing it right" in taking the advice of a young MDOT engineer in straightening the curve that existed in the old footprint and for "doing it quickly."[29] Lost in the celebration of the bridge linking Harrison and Hancock Counties together again were the deaths of three construction workers who were building the bridge. Forty-seven-year-old Steven Inscore of Wimberly, Texas, died on March 20, 2007, when the small crew boat he was piloting crashed into a barge. Fifty-one-year-old Ager Pennaman of Jackson and forty-year-old Delfino Beltran of Austin, Texas, died after plunging into the bay from a concrete platform along with six other people on June 14, 2007.[30]

Finally, while the bridge was being built, Penny Rodrique had her day in court. When she hired one of the best eminent domain attorney's in the state—Paul Scott of Smith, Phillips, Mitchell, Scott and Nowak from Hernando, Mississippi—MDOT showed its true colors. By the start of the trial on July 24, 2006, MDOT had hired a second appraiser who valued Rodrique's property not at the original offer of $416,700 but at $710,000. By its own figures, MDOT had lowballed Rodrique by almost $300,000 in its offer one month after the storm. But the story didn't end there. Rodrique hired her own appraiser and told the jury that her land and what was left of her destroyed four-thousand-square-foot building was worth $1,136,745. And after two days of testimony and short deliberations, a Harrison County jury awarded Rodrique the full amount she asked for as "just compensation."

The departure of the AmeriCorps of St. Louis from the Pass in late July 2007, nearly two years after its arrival, was bittersweet. On the one hand, the group moving on to help other towns, such as Greensburg, Kansas's tornado victims, meant that things had improved enough so that other areas of the country were in greater need. On the other hand, the group moving on was sad because it had become so ingrained in the community. The AmeriCorps is made up largely of recent college graduates. In Pass Christian, early on they helped gut homes, cut trees and remove debris from property. They also assisted in organizing and then operated the tent village after FEMA departed. As time moved on, the group got directly involved in rebuilding homes and coordinated volunteers and donations. Perhaps its longest-lasting legacy, though, is that AmeriCorps was an integral part of the *Gazebo Gazette*'s creation. Before Shmukler arrived on the coast, the group had put together a one-page newsletter with information about PODs and other things necessary for survival. Once Shmukler agreed to be the editor of an expanded newsletter, some in the AmeriCorps group gathered and reported news. In a "personal" thank-you to the AmeriCorps in the *Gazette*'s August 3, 2007 issue, Shmukler chronicled how the one-page newsletter was the early model for the *Gazette*'s first few issues. She noted that during their time reporting in Pass Christian, not a single meeting of the aldermen and other officials was missed by the newspaper. She admitted that pay back would be impossible but wrote, "I do hope some day we can pay it forward."

The U.S. Post Office reestablished itself in Pass Christian over a three-year period. Initially, temporary "cluster" boxes were set up on Espy Avenue, serving both the patrons who had boxes at the old post office destroyed by Katrina and patrons who had home delivery, which had been discontinued because conditions in the city made it impossible. In January 2006, home delivery resumed for about 350 homes in east Pass Christian. Then, in September 2006, deliveries resumed for the western portion of the Pass, including Timber Ridge, where every home was uninhabitable after Katrina. That added about 550 homes to the delivery routes in the east. Finally, on March 31, 2008, the new, smaller U.S. Post Office opened on the same footprint as the one destroyed. With the new 7,500-square-foot building came a new postmaster, Joey Cain from Gulfport. But like many things new in the Pass, Cain is connected to the rich history of the city. Cain's great-great-grandfather had been postmaster in 1868.

Not long after the post office opened its new building, on May 24, 2008, the Pass Christian Yacht Club (PCYC) became the first of the Mississippi coast yacht clubs to rebuild. Less than three months after the storm, the yacht club received approval from the city to occupy a trailer as a temporary location, first on Scenic Drive and then on the east side of the harbor. The new PCYC is about eleven thousand square feet and includes a large dining room, a boardroom and other club administrative space. Because the Pass was the location for the South's first yacht club in the mid-1800s,[31] the six-hundred-plus-member PCYC rebuilding was a huge benchmark for the harbor.

Businesses that had been in Pass Christian for decades and decided to return became an integral part of the city's recovery. Hancock Bank had offices in the city for one hundred years and had been at its current location at the corner of Scenic Drive and Market Street for over seventy-five years. Hancock had built up some additional goodwill immediately after the storm when its president, George Schloegel, authorized $200 handouts to virtually anyone who signed an IOU, customer or not. Schloegel said an unintended consequence of the generous $200 handouts loan program at all his banks on the Mississippi coast was that the goodwill garnered ultimately resulted in thirteen thousand new accounts and about a billion and a half new dollars for Hancock Bank. That growth in the five months after the storm, according to Schloegel, matched the previous ninety-five years of growth of the bank. Meanwhile, the newly renovated Hancock Bank building in downtown Pass Christian that had been heavily damaged by Katrina's winds and storm surge held its grand reopening on October 27, 2007. Among the improvements made to the 6,500-square-foot building were missile impact–resistant windows, and all electrical power lines were buried underground with connections for a portable generator in anticipation of future storms. Peoples Bank, which, like Hancock Bank, had been one of the first businesses to reopen after the storm in temporary facilities at War Memorial Park, built a new $3.5 million building downtown on Second Street. The 6,000-square-foot facility was designed to remind people of the New Orleans Garden District. The ribbon-cutting ceremony was held on December 27, 2007, and the Peoples Bank became the first brand-new building to open downtown after Hurricane Katrina.

As Labor Day approached that same year, many residents in the Pass were braced for what they feared most: another hurricane. Hurricane Gustav ended up making landfall on September 1 in neighboring Louisiana as a strong Category 2 storm with sustained winds of 110 miles per hour. Evacuations were extensive, both on the Mississippi coast and in New Orleans. Being on the eastern side of the storm, Pass Christian experienced a significant but not devastating storm surge. Only a few homes on or near North Street were flooded by the surge. Many elevated homes on pilings in Timber Ridge had water flow underneath them, and the Pass Christian Harbor had significant damage. At the peak of the storm at 3:00 p.m., there were 3,100 power outages in the Pass. The *Gazebo Gazette* reported that ten boat owners did not follow the evacuation orders, and those boats caused the bulk of the damage. However, just four days after Gustav, it was business as usual at Shaggy's restaurant, the Pass Christian Yacht Club and a gas station adjacent to the harbor, all of which reopened, though it took longer for the Department of Marine Resources to reopen oyster season.

The Pass Christian Harbor with pleasure and fishing boats. *Courtesy of Ron Daley.*

While many communities throughout the country have fought vigorously to prevent Walmart from coming, the commitment to return by the company and the ultimate rebuilding is considered an essential element to Pass Christian's survival. The city fathers held their collective breaths until Walmart publically declared it was returning to the Pass. In a February 2008 announcement, Mayor Chipper McDermott was all smiles. He called Walmart "the big horse" and declared that it was coming back to town. McDermott wanted residents to know just how important Walmart was, citing pre-Katrina monthly sales tax collections as being $110,000, with the retail giant accounting for 70 percent of that. And Walmart was planning to hire about 300 people as associates to run the rebuilt store. The retail facility was about 150,000 square feet—smaller than the original—on the same footprint as before on Highway 90 near the Long Beach line. McDermott characterized the return of Walmart as a "touchdown" for the Pass. So when the brand-new Walmart held its grand opening twenty months later on October 14, 2009, the *Gazebo Gazette* headline was hardly objective; its boosterism showed through: "Welcome Back WALMART." By the end of 2014, Walmart was back contributing 65 to 70 percent of the city's sales tax collections, about $840,000 for the year.

The Pass Christian School District—one of the best districts in the state every year—used DeLisle Elementary School and trailers set up next door after the storm until, one by one, schools were either renovated or rebuilt. First, Pass Christian High School on North Street, which had seventeen feet of water, reopened in May 2006 for the sole purpose of hosting graduation. More than 100 students attended commencement in the Pass High School gym, marking a return "home" for seniors who spent the year in portable classrooms. Pass High did not open for classes until October 2006, and the upstairs was used mostly because the classrooms on the ground floor were not quite finished. At that time, 470 students attended, down from the 620 students enrolled before Hurricane Katrina. The brand-new elementary and middle school complex at the site of the former middle school at the corner of Second Street and Church Avenue broke ground in October 2007. The $25 million campus complex also included a cafeteria and band hall, as well as a media center. The schools opened for students on August 6, 2009. Just three years later, with enrollment increasing, the district broke ground yet again, this time for a $1.5 million, 8,500-square-foot addition to the elementary school. On the same property as the elementary and middle schools, a brand-new Boys & Girls Club was built thanks to Qatar, a small but wealthy country bordering Saudi Arabia. In all, the country pledged $100 million to assist Katrina victims, and Pass Christian received $5 million to build a new Boys & Girls Club. With *Good Morning America* present and live, the ribbon cutting, which marked the opening of the new facility, was held in May 2009. The school district leases the Boys & Girls Club the land for its building, and to save money, the arrangement includes the district using the club's basketball court and gym instead of the district erecting its own school gymnasium. Meanwhile, the school district—after using the repaired DeLisle Elementary School to house students for years—eventually tore down what was left of the school and built a new elementary school complex on the same footprint. That school opened in August 2011. And finally, the new school district administration and maintenance building was built just northwest of the DeLisle Elementary School for between $2.5 and $3.0 million.

With city government operating out of trailers across from War Memorial Park, and the mayor and aldermen with their hands full just trying to help the city survive, it was a long, drawn-out process filled with difficult decisions to get permanent homes for city hall, city court, the public library and the police station. Early on, the aldermen realized that to get funding from sources such as FEMA, the Police Department and Emergency Operations Center needed to be rebuilt on high ground away from the downtown; in fact, the Emergency Operations Center was mandated by FEMA to be on land deemed on a five-hundred-year flood plain. So on October 24, 2006, the aldermen authorized eminent domain proceedings to acquire over nine acres on Espy Avenue that was over thirty feet above sea level and the only land in the city limits meeting FEMA's flood requirements. Meanwhile, the board of aldermen received all the incentive it needed to return city hall, city court and the library to their original site at the corner of Hiern Avenue and Scenic Drive; resident Dayton Robinson acquired the property immediately west of the old city hall and donated the land to the city for a municipal complex. Robinson expressed the desire for the city to eventually erect a lighthouse on the property, which had been the first structure built on the site back in 1831. On August 7, 2007, aldermen committed to returning city hall, city court and the library to the Hiern Avenue property. But it wasn't until early May 2008 that the aldermen approved the designs for the municipal complex downtown and the police headquarters and emergency ops center. In 2009, groundbreaking for the Pass Christian Public Library occurred on February 20, for the new city hall and city court on April 30 and for the new Police Department and Emergency Operations Center on Espy in August.

Flood insurance issues continue to cast a shadow over the city's ongoing recovery. And flood insurance is inextricably linked to minimum building elevations adopted by the city. Immediately after the storm, those with flood insurance were issued permits to build back at the same thirteen feet above sea level that had been in effect for decades. In October 2006, the city took a first step by raising the minimum elevation from thirteen feet above sea level in Zone A pre-Katrina to sixteen feet above sea level. This was done before FEMA had finalized its recommended flood zone map changes. By the spring of 2009, FEMA had issued its new elevation maps, and that meant Pass Christian must adopt a new ordinance and elevations so property owners would remain eligible for federally funded flood insurance. While there was leeway for the city in following some of the federal guidelines in the ordinance, the new FEMA-recommended flood elevations were adopted as is. For much of the city, the new minimum building level went from sixteen to eighteen feet above sea level. Eighteen feet became the minimum for those building homes in a flood zone, and depending on the location, some were required to build as high as twenty-two feet above sea level, with up to twenty-five feet needed if the home or business owner wanted to receive the lowest possible flood insurance premium. The new elevation maps mean that only 10 percent of the homes and businesses in the Pass are *not* in a flood zone. Meanwhile, the specter of federal flood insurance rates becoming so expensive that people can no longer afford to live in places like Pass Christian hangs over residents. The Biggert-Water Flood Insurance Reform

New Building Code ↗
22' Above Sea Level

Main Floor Height ↗
17'6" Above Sea Level

If built new today, this Timber Ridge home would need to be twenty-two feet above sea level to receive the lowest flood insurance premium. *Illustration courtesy of Wendy Roussin.*

Act of 2012—an effort to get the National Flood Insurance Program out of debt—was aimed at raising the rates dramatically for those homeowners who had their flood insurance grandfathered in under the old elevation levels. Over a five-year period, the legislation called for multifold increases in those grandfathered-in homes; some who were paying $500 to $1,000 a year would be looking at $3,000 and above per year. Action by Congress in early 2014 delayed enacting the new rates at least until the fall of 2015.

Mayor Chipper McDermott has said on numerous occasions that Pass Christian is home to the "richest of the rich and poorest of the poor." The "richest of the rich," many of whom owned homes on historic Scenic Drive, had the means to return to the Pass after Hurricane Katrina if they wanted to. But the "poorest of the poor" or even simply the lower middle class did not have those options. What brought many people other than the "richest of the rich" back were several housing developments, some federally subsidized and some not. At the corner of Cedar Avenue and North Street, Pass Estates was built. Pass Estates involves 1,300- and 2,200-square-foot, three- and four-bedroom homes that are rent-to-own. The developer, under the subsidized contract with the Mississippi Development Authority and Mississippi Home Corporation, will maintain the property for the first fifty years of its existence. Renters of the 130 homes have the option after fifteen years of occupancy of buying the homes for $50,000 with no closing costs. There are strict income requirements. The Mississippi Development Authority and Back Bay Mission teamed up to create Bethel Estates, but the development was taken over by Pass Estates when financial problems arose. Bethel Estates started out to be 32 two- and three-bedroom homes and expanded to 70 rental units in three areas of the city. These are largely rental homes, again with strict income requirements. The Cottages at Second Street comprises 40 rental homes with one-bedroom and three-bedroom units. Half the units are single-story MEMA cottages set on pilings, and the other half are two-story units on pilings, built to look like MEMA cottages. The Cottages was developed by the owner of Shaggy's, Ron Ladner, and is not federally subsidized.

The SmartCode—the new citywide zoning ordinance created and implemented after Hurricane Katrina—not only was a benchmark in the recovery of Pass Christian but also illustrated the vital role the *Gazebo Gazette* filled in the city. The newspaper covered meetings about implementing the SmartCode, it carried letters debating the SmartCode's merits and, after the code passed, city planner Jeff Bounds wrote ten information columns called "SmartCode Decoded" that the *Gazette* published, one per issue, for ten weeks. Bounds's columns detailed the intricacies of the new code and how it worked in practice. But how did the SmartCode, in practice, affect businesses in their quest to return and rebuild in the city? One word comes to mind: variances. The owners of Pirate's Cove restaurant and Live Oak Animal Hospital learned about the SmartCode intimately and claim that their rebuilding efforts were delayed and the process made much more difficult than it should have been because of the SmartCode.

For the LaMarcas, once the proposal to join Harbor Town was off the table, they looked at the possibility of returning Pirate's Cove to its original beachfront property on Highway 90. The new flood elevation requirement of twenty-two feet above sea level would have made building more expensive and access to the restaurant cumbersome. The insurance on a beachfront restaurant would have been prohibitive, anyway, with a pre-Katrina yearly cost of $20,000 ballooning to $80,000. And finally, the SmartCode requirement that businesses build close to the street or road that they are fronting would have meant that the new beachfront Pirate's Cove would be precariously close to Highway 90 on a curve where the LaMarcas' nightmares saw an eighteen-wheeler or other large vehicle round the curve and, not quite making it, crash into the restaurant. The

LaMarcas had looked at property on Menge Avenue—near the corner of Second Street—several times in the years since Hurricane Katrina. The property, compared to the beachfront before the storm and Market Street after, was off the beaten path. If they built it, would they (the customers) come? Dawn was not hesitant. She never questioned the idea that the Menge Avenue location would be successful. It took over a year of "selling" the idea to the bank, and eventually the LaMarcas had the finances in place. But then the pesky SmartCode reared its ugly head again. Because of the Menge Avenue property's size, the SmartCode would have forced them to build a really long, narrow building, given the square footage they needed for the restaurant. There were also SmartCode requirements that were at odds with the sign the LaMarcas wanted to build and the location of the building on the property. The process, Dawn said, was one big headache. However, with several variances and ultimately agreeing not to locate the new restaurant building exactly where they wanted it on the property, Pirate's Cove construction started in the spring of 2013.

For Jennifer Hendrick and Live Oak Animal Hospital, had she not been able to acquire variances, the SmartCode would have prevented her from rebuilding. First, the Peoples Bank, located at the corner of St. Louis Street and Henderson Avenue, decided not to rebuild on that property but rather to build a new bank downtown at the corner of Davis Avenue and Second Street. The land abandoned by Peoples was adjoining Hendrick's property. Hendrick eventually acquired that land, but even before she owned it, Live Oak Animal Hospital was operating on it in a used rented sixteen- by seventy-two-foot trailer. The planning process for a new facility started in 2008, and immediately Hendrick had to navigate around the SmartCode. The code essentially called for a building in downtown (which her location was, according to the code, although she didn't consider it to be) to be ten to fifteen feet from the street. She wanted a parking lot "fronting" St. Louis, so she had to break one parcel of land into two, with the front "vacant" parcel used for the parking lot and the second parcel used for the new hospital with the "front" now on Henderson Avenue instead of St. Louis. There were variances or rezoning required to work around the requirement of building two stories high and to be allowed farther away from Henderson than required because of an oak tree on the property. Finally, FEMA approved building back at seventeen feet above sea level. Construction started on the new Live Oak Animal Hospital in 2009.

By the summer of 2009, business owners in the Pass were not happy with the pace of recovery. So a group headed by the owner of Shaggy's restaurant and the Cottages developer, Ron Ladner, paid for nationally known architect and planner Andres Duany to come to the city and, with input from property owners, create a detailed plan for the downtown redevelopment. Mayor Chipper McDermott remembers like it was yesterday one of the first things Duany said upon arrival. Duany observed that the city was closer to its condition in the 1850s than anytime during the twentieth or twenty-first centuries. According to Duany, whose name is linked closely to the concept of a SmartCode, that meant development would have to be in increments rather than trying to build back perfectly. Duany seemed to imply that the rigid standards of the SmartCode needed to take a backseat to smaller-scale buildings that would serve as "incubators" for retail and restaurants. Duany also stressed that building in less expensive ways with canopy-covered open-air restaurants and low-cost modular buildings on Scenic Drive, Davis Avenue and Market Street would promote retail. Even the SmartCode's biggest proponent, city planner Jeff Bounds, understood Duany's vision and the reasoning behind it. In a *Gazebo Gazette* column from August 21, 2009, summarizing the "Top Five Ideas from the Downtown Charrette," Bounds wrote that he originally "believed the choice was between no standards or high standards," but now the possibility was raised for "low-cost build-outs for the near term" while still ensuring uniformity in the downtown as demand increased. Duany specifically recommended allowing construction of functional buildings that would be contrary to the SmartCode, which would be in place for eight years to allow a retail presence to be reestablished. The overarching theme was that the city needed to do everything it could to get businesses back in the short term and then the long term would take care of itself.

By January 2010, the board of aldermen had perhaps realized that strict adherence to the SmartCode was stifling new business creation in the downtown. Some of Duany's advice clearly turned into policy. The aldermen created a "transitional recovery overlay" zone in parts of the downtown that effectively relaxed portions of the SmartCode. Specifically, the transitional zone allowed for the building of one-story structures rather than two stories as T-5 designated areas required, and interior twelve-foot ceiling height minimums were waived. Further, some exteriors that were forbidden, such as stucco and metal siding, were allowed, and multiple smaller buildings would be allowed on one parcel instead of two maximum under the SmartCode. With the aldermen's action, the temporary zone is in effect until December 31, 2018, at which time the buildings will have to be removed or brought up to code. Some city officials predicted that building in the new transitional zone would cost about half of what the SmartCode had been dictating.

The relaxing of the SmartCode ultimately led to the largest singular commercial development in Pass Christian post Hurricane Katrina, and it grew out of the existing Martin Hardware on Davis Avenue. Founded in 1932 by Charlie Martin, the hardware store stayed in the Martin family for decades. Jim and Doreen Grotkowski purchased it in 2004. Hurricane Katrina destroyed it, and the Grotkowskis rebuilt, reopening in May 2006. The new commercial development was called Martin Plaza and included the hardware store, Subway, Pass Wine and Spirits and Blue Skies Gallery. When Grotkowski decided to sell so he could pursue some other opportunities in Florida, Adam Pace and his partners, Ben Puckett Sr. and Ben Puckett Jr., stepped in. After Katrina, Pace, who was attending the University of Southern Mississippi, returned to Long Beach to help put the family home back together while living in a camper. He never returned to USM. Pace eventually went to work for Weyerhaeuser but was helping design homes in places other than the coast. As the coast was trying to come back from Katrina, Pace left Weyerhaeuser, worked with the Pass in the planning department and later became self-employed looking at vacant land for economic development opportunities. Pace, with the assistance of Mayor Chipper McDermott, bought a 120- by 121-foot parcel of land immediately north of Martin Hardware for $150,000 from Hancock Bank. That turned out to be the first step in a three-step process that resulted in a commercial square in downtown Pass Christian. Pace and the Pucketts formed the Sazerac Group and, in November 2010, purchased Martin Plaza. The name of the group is a tribute to the first bar in Pass Christian, the Sazerac Saloon, which once occupied the same property. Less than a year later, in August 2011, construction began on what was named Sazerac Square, seamlessly connected to Martin Plaza. The new development was six buildings—some stick-built and others former MEMA cottages—tied together by a large wooden deck. Pace was a realist, admitting that part of the reason MEMA cottages were used was his "exit strategy." The MEMA cottages would be easy to move and possibly resell if the development went belly up. The development, which has become the hub of Pass Christian's downtown with fourteen businesses, would never have happened if the SmartCode had not been relaxed. In taking advantage of the city's "transitional" building program that waived the two-story building requirement, among other things, and the city's tax abatement program that allowed developers to pay property tax on the land and not the buildings, the city helped foster creating businesses that otherwise would not have been. Sazerac Square is a prime example.

To be accurate, the SmartCode has plenty of supporters and, in the long term, may serve the city well. Mississippi Coast Realty owner Ken Austin—who, besides being 2009 Realtor of the Year in the state, has held many positions on boards and commissions in the city over the years, including being on the planning commission—admits the two-story requirement of the SmartCode may have been "too aggressive," but lack of available capital and the high cost of insurance are the main reasons business growth has been slow. Two other main reasons are the economic recession and the BP oil spill, according to Austin. But he says it is "patently" incorrect to single out the SmartCode as stifling development, and he called it a "viable, working, living document that has changed and adapted to meet the specific needs of the community, rather than a rigid, never-changing law or ordinance."[32]

After Hurricane Katrina, the Scenic Drive location that St. Paul Catholic Church had occupied for over 150 years was the cause of much angst by parishioners and city officials for nearly eight years. For most of those eight years, only a large steel cross stood on the vacant prime beachfront land. St. Paul's was one of ten churches essentially destroyed in the Catholic Diocese of Biloxi. Perhaps the first step in what became years of contentious relations between some of St. Paul's parishioners and the church was November 27, 2005, the first Sunday of Advent, when Our Lady of Lourdes Parish was combined with St. Paul Parish to form the new Holy Family Parish. Bishop Thomas J. Rodi appointed Father Dennis J. Carver as the first pastor. Rodi had met with St. Paul's parishioners about their church's future in early October 2005 and said he planned to meet similarly with other parishes before making rebuilding decisions. And, in late October, Father Carver held what he called a homecoming service in the battered A-frame shell of a church that St. Paul's parishioners had called home since 1972. At that homecoming service, it was still very much up in the air what the diocese was going to do about rebuilding. A hint of what was to occur came in February 2006, when Bishop Rodi announced that the elementary schools in Pass Christian and Long Beach, which had held joint operations after the storm, would merge and a new school be built off Menge Avenue just outside the city limits where Our Lady of Lourdes Parish Church stood. In August 2006, students from both schools came together in "new" temporary facilities, which included portable or modular classrooms, on the twenty-three-acre Menge Avenue property.

In March 2007, Father Carver announced that the battered old St. Paul's Church on the beachfront would be converted into a community center and the new Holy Family Parish Church would be built on the Menge Avenue property, essentially out of harm's way. Reaction came fast from Pass Christian's city fathers. Mayor Chipper McDermott, known to speak his mind regardless of the consequences, told the *Gazebo Gazette* at the time that moving the location of a "165-year-old church and a 158-year-old school" from the center of town was an "absolute disgrace."[33] Meanwhile, in the March 16 issue, the *Gazette*'s coverage of the decision, titled "St. Paul Church Decision: The Public and Parish React," reflected outrage like no other issue before or after. Jesse Heitzmann wrote that abandoning the Scenic Drive church seemed "unthinkable" and that "when the church should be actively supporting a return to normalcy, it seems to be adding to the upheaval." Anne Tucker wrote that the church sought donations from all over the country for "THE REBUILDING OF ST. PAUL'S CATHOLIC CHURCH" not building a new church at a different location. Frank Schmidt Sr. admitted that the "super-slide" A-framed church erected after Hurricane Camille was a shock to many people but "came to be loved by the people, like a little ugly pup that becomes your faithful companion." Wendy Allard called the plans to turn the church into a community center and build a new church a "waste of resources," and Maggie Marquez-Wooten wrote that returning St. Paul to its original location was the "only right thing to do." However, one letter writer, R. Carousel, took the mayor to task for complaining about the church spending $17 million for a new church and civic center. Carousel noted the city still did not have a "major grocery store, restaurant, and pharmacy" and that "debris still resides in the drainage ditches," and he asked, "Great going Mayor—what next?"

Conceding that her newspaper was not a "pulpit," Evelina Shmukler wrote, "We must keep the faith." Noting that her office in the Colonnade Building was right next door to the St. Paul's property, she wrote in the April 13, 2007 *Gazette* that she was "saddened" that the church had chosen not to rebuild downtown but that a community center was better than nothing. Her message, though, was about the big picture: "If an organization with the pooled resources of the Catholic Church chooses to leave downtown, where does that leave the rest of us—those of us without 1.1 billion members to back us up?" Opponents of moving the church were persistent with rallies in late March and early April 2007; the creation of a website, www.savestpauls. com; and the donation of a silver 1982 Chevrolet Corvette by Ralph Ladner to be raffled off to raise money to save the church. Then, on May 1, 2007, a group of about 150 parishioners filed suit in Chancery Court in Gulfport. The group asked for the court to determine the bishop and parish priest's "sacred" obligation to keep the Scenic Drive property for a church, to question turning a church into a community center and to get an accounting for monies donated to rebuild St. Paul's. The week after the lawsuit was filed, Bishop Rodi issued a statement that the *Gazebo Gazette* published in its entirety, along with a news story that summarized the statement. Rodi challenged the lawsuit under numerous grounds, not the least of which was that a court order would violate the Constitution's First Amendment, separation of church and state. He also called the suit an attack on "both the unity and liberty of the Church."[34] One of the most prominent opposition voices was Frank Schmidt Sr. Besides the lawsuit, Schmidt submitted numerous letters to the editor in the *Gazette*, including one with pictures to go along with it on October 12, 2007. Schmidt said essentially that razing St. Paul's after Hurricane Katrina was history repeating itself with what the diocese did after Hurricane Camille. Three pictures of the old St. Paul's immediately after Camille show a church that appeared to be salvable. Schmidt claimed it was repairable; instead, it was demolished by order of the pastor, and the A-frame was built, opening in 1972. Schmidt wrote that the same was being done after Hurricane Katrina; the shell of St. Paul's remained and could be rebuilt, but the pastor ordered that it be converted into a community center.

In March 2008, Chancery Court dismissed the lawsuit on the grounds that the court had no jurisdiction, and the plaintiffs immediately appealed to the Mississippi Supreme Court. While appealing the decision, the Save St. Paul's organization continued its campaign. In September 2009, the State Supreme Court ruled that the land, buildings and insurance settlement belonged to Holy Family Parish but left the door open for the lower court to hear complaints about the money collected to rebuild St. Paul's, which made the plaintiffs hopeful an out-of-court settlement could be reached. However, nearly one year later, in August 2010, the Diocese of Biloxi announced that St. Paul's would be demolished. And in what seemed like the spirit of compromise, the new bishop, Roger Morin, mentioned the possibility of raising funds for a one-hundred-seat chapel to sit on the church's Scenic Drive property—but only after the new Holy Family Parish Church was built on Menge.

Nothing came easy in this eight-year struggle. The Pass Christian Historical Preservation Committee, after a heavily attended public hearing, voted unanimously in November 2010, to deny a permit to tear down what was left of St. Paul's. The committee decided that the cultural significance of the building warranted saving it. In the church's appeal of the decision to the Pass Christian Board of Aldermen, it argued that St. Paul's hurricane-gutted A-frame represented "no redeemable architectural and historical significance." No sooner did aldermen vote to overturn the Historical Preservation Committee's decision than Mayor Chipper McDermott vetoed the church's demolition, demanding to know from the diocese what its plans were for the Scenic Drive property. Years later, McDermott said he was fighting as hard as he could for the survival of Pass Christian and felt that St. Paul's Church, in the heart of the downtown, brought four hundred people for services every Sunday, four hundred people who wouldn't be downtown otherwise. Before the aldermen took a vote on whether to override the mayor's veto, a diocese attorney committed the church to building a chapel-of-ease on the vacant land. The aldermen then gave the go-ahead to tear down St. Paul's. And despite an appeal for a stay filed by Save St. Paul's in Harrison County Circuit Court, on December 20, 2010, the shell of what once was St. Paul's Church was torn down, with only a large steel cross remaining on the property. Litigation continued, not about the demolition, but about where the money went that was collected by the diocese to rebuild St. Paul's. Disgruntled parishioner Jesse Heitzmann's letter in the January 7, 2011 *Gazette* said that the promise to build a chapel on the old St. Paul's property with newly raised money added "insult to injury" and declared that "those responsible for the demise of St. Paul are destined to carry the burden of this betrayal with them whatever they do and wherever they may eventually go." Mayor Chipper McDermott observed that in the end, "fighting city hall's tough. Fighting Italy is a lot harder."[35]

On January 25, 2014, the new 13,000-square-foot Holy Family Catholic Church that seats four hundred was dedicated in its Menge Avenue location. The new chapel-of-ease, designed to look like the St. Paul Church that existed before Hurricane Camille, was likewise finished in March 2014. The 2,500-square-foot chapel that seats about one hundred people and the old steel cross are all that sits on the 4.25-acre Scenic Drive property, which before Hurricane Katrina was the home to St. Paul's Church and rectory and the St. Paul's Elementary School. The dispute between the Catholic Church and the Save St. Paul group about where the money collected to rebuild St. Paul was allocated made its way to the Mississippi State Supreme Court. In a July 17, 2014 ruling,

St. Paul Chapel-of-Ease located on Scenic Drive in Pass Christian.

the high court found for the Catholic Diocese of Biloxi: "Because none of the Plaintiffs established the requisite elements for a diversion of designated funds, we affirm the grant of summary judgment on this issue. In addition, because no Plaintiffs could establish a claim for intentional misrepresentation, we affirm the grant of summary judgment on this issue." Reverend Roger Morin, bishop of Biloxi Diocese, had decided that the new chapel-of-ease would not be opened or used on a regular basis until there were no longer legal proceedings. The chapel then sat there vacant, except on a special-permission basis, until a couple of weeks after the Supreme Court ruling, when a regular schedule was established. The first official Mass was on July 30, 2014, and in a statement about the litigation, Morin said, "Let us commit to moving ahead as a community of Christian believers who are recognized by the charity we practice and the love that we show for one another."[36]

Another church with a long history in Pass Christian, Trinity Episcopal, had its own issues in building back on a site it had occupied since 1849. Immediately after the storm, Reverend Christopher Colby told the church board that planning to rebuild Trinity was premature; the first step was rebuilding the city. As time went by and the city stabilized, only about 40 percent of the Trinity congregation returned. Colby started working with an architect who came up with a plan to have two working buildings. However, when the process seemed to be moving at a glacial pace, a group at the church took over the building committee, hired a different architect and developed a plan that involved only one building. While Trinity never suffered through a fight in the courts like St. Paul's Catholic Church, the disagreement between Colby and church members was bitter, with Colby feeling "violated" in having the rebuilding authority yanked from him. Nevertheless, in May 2009, one of the first major steps in rebuilding Trinity Church occurred with the raising of the three-thousand-square-foot shell that was the sanctuary to twelve feet above the ground. Having been a presence in Pass Christian for over 150 years, the raising of the sanctuary constituted a major event in the city, even though that particular church had been in existence only since after Hurricane Camille. During the first week of March 2010, church members and guests returned to Trinity for the first services in the renovated/rebuilt sanctuary. The "new" church included two extended two-story additions attached to the original sanctuary. Bishop Duncan M. Gray held the official rededication ceremony on April 28, 2010. Reverend Colby has since retired from Trinity, and in February 2014, he was named by city aldermen to fill a vacancy on the Pass Christian School District Board of Trustees.

The First Baptist Church on Second Street received seemingly unprecedented help, not only from the Mississippi Baptist Convention and other Baptists around the country but also from countless other organizations, from the Amish to AmeriCorps. In all, First Baptist received between $80,000 and $85,000 in insurance. Renovating the education building cost about $65,000. That left $15,000 to $20,000. The sanctuary was $500,000 in materials alone and a new children's building cost about $473,000, which, except for the remaining insurance money, came from donations big and small. The church moved into its new sanctuary in December 2008, and once the sanctuary was completely finished, a special dedication service was held on March 8, 2009. The church was originally built in 1929. The rebuild was done like that of almost every other church damaged—through volunteers from all over the country. The church survived despite having only seventeen members in the congregation immediately after Hurricane Katrina.

Every church in Pass Christian received damage, ranging from destroyed to relatively minor flooding. The Goodwill Missionary Baptist Church on Davis Avenue suffered from about twenty-five feet of water from Katrina's surge. Churches from around the country pitched in to help Goodwill repair its facility, and on July 23, 2006—less than a year after the storm—rededication services were held with more than three hundred people attending. Our Mother of Mercy Catholic Church had its sanctuary and school building damaged heavily, and its rectory was destroyed. On Sunday, June 10, 2007, the first service inside the church after Hurricane Katrina was held. The Josephite priests, who are dedicated to serving the African American community, built Mother of Mercy in 1911, and though heavily damaged by Hurricane Camille and Hurricane Katrina, it survived both. First Missionary Baptist Church on Clarke Avenue was destroyed and deemed structurally unsound to rebuild. The church was demolished, and then on May 5, 2013—nearly seven years after Katrina—services were held in the congregation's new facility. In 2015, the church will celebrate 145 years of service in Pass Christian.

Pass Christian is nothing if not proud of its history. The Pass Christian Historical Society claims the Blue Rose on Scenic Drive across Highway 90 from the harbor is the oldest beachfront home in the city. The Blue Rose was built in 1848 and has survived every hurricane since, including Hurricane Katrina. In 1990, Philip LaGrange opened the Blue Rose as a restaurant, and it stayed open until 1998. Then in 2004, LaGrange opened up again for weekend dining and as a bed-and-breakfast. Off and on over the years, the Blue Rose has been a restaurant, bed-and-breakfast and antiques store. After Katrina, owners LaGrange and his partner, Herb Pursley, surveyed the damage, and even with the walls blown out, the front porch collapsed and a tree up against its side, they decided to rebuild. At one point, they reopened for special events but then shut down because of spiraling insurance costs. At that time, they put the Blue Rose up for sale. In November 2008, with still no buyers, they reopened for special events, including weddings and anniversaries. One big change in the Blue Rose with the rebuild was that it was no longer blue. LaGrange and Pursley decided to go with a cream color, which matches closely what the home looked like when it was originally constructed in the mid-1800s.

Chapter 6

Transition

The Gazette *Comes to a Crossroads*

I am so happy that this transition is going to allow me to remain a citizen
of our remarkable city.
—*Evelina* [Shmukler] *Burnett*

During the summer of 2012, Evelina Shmukler decided to publish on an every-other-week schedule. But as fall and winter rolled by, the *Gazebo Gazette* remained on this schedule for the first extended period of time in its six-and-a-half-year existence. The reduced publication schedule was actually years in the making.

When Shmukler relocated to Pass Christian permanently in May 2006, she was single and had had the talent and good fortune to have worked in the media and reported from various parts around the world. Moving to the Pass was another adventure fulfilling an unending curiosity. Then, when she found that as a journalist she could make a difference and be part of Pass Christian's recovery, she stayed. Over the *Gazebo Gazette*'s first five years, Shmukler "bonded" with the city and developed close relationships with officials and citizens trying to bring the city back from ruin. After the city stabilized, the *Gazette* needed to transition to a more traditional newspaper from a "booster," and that was difficult for Shmukler.

In retrospect, she remembers a particularly bitter fight about whether Erin and Chase Moseley's home at 855 East Scenic Drive could be operated as a bed-and-breakfast. In September 2010, the Moseleys argued that under the 1970 code, a bed-and-breakfast could be allowed by special exception, while neighbors argued bed-and-breakfasts were not allowed under any conditions. Those opposed argued that it would be a bad precedent to allow a commercial bed-and-breakfast in a residential neighborhood and, further, that a bed-and-breakfast would hurt property values in the homes around it. Ultimately, the Pass Christian Zoning Board of Appeals approved the application, but not before Shmukler noticed something very different going on in the city. There had been many controversial debated topics and decisions up to that time in rebuilding the Pass, but the give-and-take was largely on the merits of the issue, not based on personal attacks. Shmukler noted that the debate over the bed-and-breakfast marked a transition in the recovery from togetherness in the face of disagreement to opposition by "vitriolic" attacks.[37] She remembers how painful it was to report on controversial issues because the newspaper was founded on the premise that citizens needed information to give them hope that the city could come back.

So while the city was evolving and getting closer to "normalcy," Shmukler and her husband, Paul Burnett, became parents with the birth of a son, Sam, on August 31, 2011. From September through December 2011, the *Gazebo Gazette*'s version of maternity leave was for Shmukler to publish every other week instead of every week. On the first of the year in 2012, the *Gazette* went back to weekly, but in June, Shmukler announced a summer schedule of every other week, which ended up as the schedule until she sold the paper in May 2013.

The desire to spend more time with her family and the reality that the newspaper was really only breaking even were two reasons that Shmukler needed to let her baby—that is, her first baby, the *Gazette*—go. Shmukler's attachment to the city and its citizens as the city struggled to recover after Katrina was not allowing her to do it justice in reporting on divisive issues. So in the spring of 2013, she interviewed with and was offered and accepted a position with Mississippi Public Broadcasting as a reporter on the coast. Clearly, publishing the *Gazebo Gazette* in and of itself was more than a full-time job, so something would have to give.

Enter Jace R. Ponder, son of *Sea Coast Echo* publisher James "Randy" Ponder. The younger Ponder was born with ink in his veins. His father had been in the newspaper business as a publisher and editor for many years, his uncle published a paper in North Alabama and three of his cousins were all in the newspaper business in some shape or form.

Ponder remembers vividly the ink-and-paper smell in the printing press room of the *Echo*. At an early age, the younger Ponder would accompany his father covering high school football games, holding the camera case and later taking pictures with the newspaper's 35mm Nikon camera. But as a

Publisher and editor of the *Gazebo Gazette* Jace Ponder covers the christening of the new Pass Christian Harbor, July 22, 2014.

teenager, following his father around and being a newspaper "cub" reporter wasn't in the cards. Ponder had very little to do with his father's newspaper. As he entered college, he decided that physics would be his major at the University of Southern Mississippi in Hattiesburg, but he quickly found doing research alone in a laboratory with very little human contact was not for him. Three semesters in, Ponder dropped out in 2005. Needing a job, his father hired him as a typesetter with the *Echo*; he was the low man on the totem pole doing rewrites of press releases and writing obituaries. Then, on August 29, 2005, Hurricane Katrina hit. The *Sea Coast Echo* was totally destroyed, but after the elder Ponder quickly made arrangements to have the newspaper printed just north at the *Picayune Item*, everyone on staff became a reporter. The younger Ponder was no longer tied to the printing press and office; he was riding his bicycle everywhere, fleshing out stories and taking all the photographs to go with them. Ponder recalls a few days after the storm taking a long ride out to unincorporated Hancock County's Clermont Harbor and the Lakeshore community—a considerable distance from the centers of Bay St. Louis and Waveland. The residents who survived Katrina were totally cut off from the world. As Ponder took photographs and gathered information for stories, he passed out copies of the *Echo*. He remembers tears in many of the people's eyes; they finally had a link to other residents and could get a grasp on what was going on. The National Guard literally did not know there were survivors in Clermont Harbor and Lakeshore, and as Ponder left, he promised to make sure they were not forgotten by personally informing the National Guard. Ponder thought to himself that this was what community journalism was all about.

Nevertheless, after reporting on the initial crisis caused by Hurricane Katrina, Ponder left the *Echo* and spent several months as an AmeriCorps community service worker. When Ponder left AmeriCorps, he traveled around the country for a couple of years "drifting." In the summer of 2007, while sitting on a beach on the coast of Maine, Ponder had a moment of clarity: journalism was the profession for him after all. He enrolled at the University of Mississippi in Oxford and registered for every semester—fall, winter intercession, spring, summer and summer intercession—completing his bachelor's degree in 2009 and finishing the coursework, but not the thesis, for a master's degree in 2010. Ponder returned to Bay St. Louis, and with no positions open at the *Sea Coast Echo*, he took a job at the Bay St. Louis Public Library. Finally, in 2012, he was hired at the *Echo* as a reporter and sales representative. In his position, he would see Evelina Shmukler when she came to pick up copies of the *Gazebo Gazette*, which she had printed by the *Sea Coast Echo*. In fact, Shmukler approached Randy Ponder about selling the *Gazette* to the *Echo* early in 2013. The elder Ponder decided the financials were such that he did not want to take on the paper from neighboring Pass Christian. But Jace Ponder liked the newspaper and was ready for a new challenge. He talked with Shmukler and quickly purchased the *Gazette* for what he termed a "fair price." In June, his first month as the *Gazebo Gazette*'s editor and publisher, he worked day and night because he kept his job with the *Sea Coast Echo*. Starting in midsummer of 2013, Ponder left the *Echo* and was on his own.

Evelina (Shmukler) Burnett looking at her last issue of the *Gazebo Gazette* as editor and publisher.

For Shmukler, in just over seven years, she had gone from reporting on Hurricane Katrina to one of thousands of volunteers who came to the Pass to a permanent fixture as publisher of the *Gazette*. Virtually everyone in the city had come to know her, either directly or through reading and hearing about the *Gazette*. In passing the baton to Ponder, Shmukler wrote a letter to readers titled "Changes at the *Gazebo Gazette*," which appeared on the front page of her last issue, May 17 and May 24, 2013. She wrote that she was honored to have been editor and publisher over the years since Katrina, "watching the regrowth and resilience of this remarkable community." Citing the growth of her family—she had gotten married and had a child— and a new professional opportunity, she made one of the "hardest decisions" in her life in letting the newspaper go. She predicted the *Gazette* would become even "better and stronger" than it currently was, suggesting that the new owner would return to weekly publishing and that more hard news and sports coverage was expected. She wrote that Pass Christian was "happily" a "very different" place than it had been when she started the *Gazette* in 2006 and that the city "now requires a different type of newspaper." Shmukler was certain that the new owner would "remain committed to the core principle of the *Gazebo Gazette*, which is to provide news that is for and about our small, special community." Fitting to her reign as editor and publisher and the *Gazette*'s founding principles, her last issue featured five full pages of transcripts from interviews with the candidates for mayor and board of aldermen in the upcoming June 4 election. The *Gazebo Gazette* was doing what it had done since the very first issue on January 13, 2006: providing residents detailed information not available anywhere else that would help them make important decisions about the men and women who would lead the city.

Conclusion

PASS CHRISTIAN TODAY

We have the richest rich, poorest of poor....Down at that harbor right there, they speak four languages; French, Spanish, English and Vietnamese.
—*Mayor Chipper McDermott*

The 2013 U.S. census figures have Pass Christian's population at 5,128, up over 11.00 percent from 2010 and 3.55 percent from 2012, making it the eighth fastest-growing city in the state. Of course, coast cities, including Bay St. Louis, D'Iberville and Ocean Springs, are still well short of their pre–Hurricane Katrina population figures. Pass Christian mayor Chipper McDermott credits the increase in his city to the top-rated public school system and the construction of several subdivisions built with post-Katrina relief money. However, the population was about 6,655 in 2005, the year Hurricane Katrina hit. So the Pass remains the city on the coast with the largest percentage of lost population. Nearby Waveland has the second-largest loss in population due to Hurricane Katrina.[38]

Even thirty-five years after Hurricane Camille, the locals could point to empty lots and slabs and tell you whose business used to be here or who lived there before. So it is to no one's surprise that nearly ten years after Hurricane Katrina there are still many reminders of what once was. Driving along historic Highway 90 in the Pass, there are very few residences bordering the highway any longer; instead, there are "For Sale" signs on lots that people have decided not to build back on. There are many slabs where homes once were, and the closer the neighborhood is to Highway 90, the more you see empty lots. For instance, the front steps to a home that no longer exists and an overgrown

The Pass Christian welcome sign.

swimming pool remain on a St. Louis Street lot that used to be the home of Helen and Nelson Lang, seventy-two and seventy-six years of age, respectively. The Langs, both with failing health, decided that since their home had survived Hurricane Camille, it most certainly could handle any future hurricane. Instead, their home crumbled in the surge, and both died. Their bodies were found in the rubble near the railroad tracks behind their home. To those who knew the Langs—and that includes nearly all city residents—the steps to nowhere remain an unending reminder of the couple's untimely death. But not all the reminders are as macabre as vacant slabs where homes once were and steps to homes of the dead. On 118 Fairway Drive in Timber Ridge—where every home was either destroyed or flooded to the point of being uninhabitable—a mailbox from 106 Fairway Drive remains high in a tree. The home at 118 Fairway has a different owner than when Katrina hit, but the new owners have left that mailbox in the tree all these years.

Another constant reminder of Hurricane Katrina is the dozens of people who rebuilt their homes, or bought rebuilt homes, who now have dumpsters and storage PODS outside their homes as they perform yet another rebuild. Many of them are victims of the second tragedy of property damage after

Slabs where homes once stood are common, particularly in the lower-lying western portion of Pass Christian. This one is on Clarence Avenue.

Helen and Nelson Lang were killed when the surge washed away their home. The stairs are a constant reminder.

Number 118 Fairway Drive with the mailbox from 106 Fairway Drive still in a tree nine years after Hurricane Katrina.

Hurricane Katrina: the homes they own were rebuilt with toxic Chinese drywall. The drywall was imported between 2001 and 2007 and contained metals and minerals such as sulfur, strontium and iron. Under certain conditions, including the warm, humid climate in the South, the drywall emits an odor and corrodes copper and other metal surfaces. Most of the homeowners' affected reported air conditioners, appliances and other electronics failing, and many suffered from allergies and other maladies. There is a formal test done to confirm or deny defective Chinese drywall, but telltale signs are obvious: black mold on copper pipes or exposed copper wires almost certainly means bad drywall. New Orleans firefighter George Marshall had been coming to the Mississippi coast from the Crescent City since he was twelve years old. Like many New Orleanians, his father owned a camp on the coast. Marshall took three years to rebuild that camp after Hurricane Katrina's surge filled it to the peak. As living conditions deteriorated in New Orleans, Marshall and his wife, Beth, contemplated moving to the coast, and after Beth secured a job in Gulfport, the Marshalls bought a 1,400-square-foot home with three bedrooms on Poinsettia Loop in Timber Ridge, with a view of the Pass Christian Isles Golf Club's seventeenth hole just off the back porch. Oddly, a stranger Marshall met at a casino who recommended looking in Timber Ridge for a home turned out to become his new next-door neighbor on Poinsettia Loop. Meanwhile, the Marshalls poured $28,000 into improvements to get the home just about where they wanted it. Then, an attorney on one of the class action Chinese drywall lawsuits called and told them that records showed that when their home was rebuilt after Katrina, toxic drywall from China was used. They had experienced no symptoms. Upon further inspection, though, even though the home had flooded just three feet, so only four feet of drywall was replaced, the toxic mold had caused corrosion on everything metal. The home was stripped of everything except the two-by-four studs and rebuilt. During the rebuild, the Marshalls stayed in the old family camp. They moved back in their home in October 2013. Marshall says the lawsuit covered everything in the rebuild to the tune of about $130,000. And Marshall has no regrets in moving to the Pass: "This is where I'm dying."[39]

According to the Pass Christian Building Code Enforcement office, officially thirty-six homes in the city have been rebuilt because of toxic Chinese drywall as of the summer of 2014. Among those is former alderman Huey Bang's home. Bang spent years and years waiting for class action litigation to make its way through the courts before moving back into his home on Redbud Way in March 2014 after the home's second rebuild since Katrina. Likewise, owner of Live Oak Animal Hospital, Jennifer Hendrick, and her husband, Scott Niolet, were part of a class action lawsuit that led to their home off Demourelle being rebuilt. They moved back to their rebuilt home in the summer of 2014. Because there has been no scientific evidence of long-term health effects from Chinese drywall, many homeowners, including Bang and his family and Hendrick and Niolet, stayed in their homes until the litigation made its way through the legal system and they got the go ahead to rebuild. However, Niolet did experience migraine headaches and sinus issues he attributes to the tainted drywall. About 90 percent of the Mississippians who had defective Chinese drywall got closure from a settlement on February 7, 2013. On that date, a federal judge approved five class action suit settlements, with the biggest culprit being Knauf Plasterboard Drywall, which reportedly was involved in 4,500 homes nationwide and 700 in Mississippi alone. Chinese-based Taishan fought the lawsuits on the grounds that U.S. courts had no jurisdiction over a company based in China. The Fifth Circuit Court of Appeals upheld the U.S. court jurisdiction in the case in January 2014, but other appeals are still pending.

Some of the businesses that decided not to return to Pass Christian are national chains that are so common elsewhere they are hardly missed. McDonald's, Domino's and Rite Aid were convenient to have in the Pass and helped with the city's fragile tax collections, but they do not provoke sadness in residents because they didn't return. The Miramar Lodge Nursing Home and Twin Oaks Assisted Living facility provided employment to a good number of people and served the community's elderly well. But they have not returned, and no similar facilities have been built since the storm. In other cases, Pass Christian's loss has been other coast cities' gain. For instance, the highly successful Harbor View Café that had operated on Highway 90 across from the harbor—thus the name—relocated to Long Beach and opened up a brand-new restaurant in 2011 one block from the beach. The Hillyer House, which featured artistic jewelry, pottery and creative gifts, had been in the Pass since 1970, but after being destroyed by Katrina, it eventually relocated permanently to the vibrant Ocean Springs downtown on the eastern portion of the Mississippi Gulf Coast. Ironically, the Hillyer House was created after Hurricane Camille to help people replace necessities such as furniture and other household items. After a number of phases, Hillyer House morphed in the mid-1980s into carrying the work of highly respected American artists and eventually featuring local and regional artists' wares. That motif fit nicely into the largely undamaged Ocean Springs downtown.

There are reminders of Hurricane Katrina that are positive—turning lemons into lemonade if you will. On Highway 90, for decades to come, people will admire coast-themed chainsaw sculptures in the median from Waveland in the west to Biloxi in the east, including Pass Christian. These are borne from oak trees that did not survive the storm. Initially, the

Mississippi Department of Transportation (MDOT) bulldozed many of the dead oak trees in preparation for rebuilding Highway 90, but public outcry led to stripping the trees of their branches and leaving them to become the artwork of sculptors, such as Marlin Miller of Fort Walton Beach, Florida, and Dayton Scoggins of Sandersville, Mississippi. Miller did many of the pieces on the coast, including a large eagle, which is located in the city's War Memorial Park and dedicated to Colonel Lawrence E. Roberts, a Tuskegee

The eagle carved in an oak tree by Marlin Miller in War Memorial Park, dedicated to former Tuskegee Airman Colonel Lawrence E. Roberts.

Oak tree art carved by Dayton Scoggins on the median of Highway 90 in Pass Christian.

Airman and father of *Good Morning America*'s Robin Roberts. Scoggins was also very active, and his creations include a dolphins and fish carving on a dead oak tree across from city hall on the Highway 90 median.

Specifically, how is the Pass Christian School District doing these days? A May 14, 2014 story in the state's largest-circulation newspaper, the *Clarion-Ledger*, told it all with the headline "Pass Christian as Academic Powerhouse." The article revealed that in the two months the schools were not in session after Hurricane Katrina, administrators held a retreat and decided on a simple mission statement: "Commitment to excellence." Superintendent

Beth John told the newspaper that by every district employee having a stake in the students' success—including the bus drivers, who wanted to know when important state tests were being administered so they could encourage the students—they would be "living our beliefs."[40] Living their beliefs, the Pass Christian School District has been rated number one in Mississippi for five consecutive years. In the 2004–05 academic year, 1,980 students were enrolled in Pass Christian schools. That plummeted by more than 30 percent, down to 1,343 students for the 2005–06 school year. For the most recent 2014–15 academic year, enrollment climbed to 2,007 students, which means nine years later, enrollment has exceeded pre-Katrina levels for the first time. The poverty level of the district, as measured by the free and reduced lunch count, is about 64 percent, which is slightly lower than before the storm. The per pupil expenditure is about $12,500, well above the state average of about $8,700. Business manager Marsha Garziano said the one thing they learned from the storm and the district's ability to sustain high standards in adverse conditions was that "the school is not the buildings; it's the people."[41]

Many of the locally owned businesses that were in the city before the storm are thriving a decade later. At Pirate's Cove, once it reopened in the new building on Menge Avenue, everything fell into place. The restaurant employs twenty-five to forty people at any one time, with fourteen people on duty during busy shifts. It does about a fifty-fifty split between those who dine in and those who have take-out. The Fourth of July 2014 was a record sales day for Pirate's Cove, with constant orders from when it opened at 10:00 a.m. until it closed. Dawn LaMarca says the crew was so tired that instead of making sandwiches to eat after closing on the Fourth, she sent out for pizza. They could not make one more sandwich. She is already talking about franchising the Pirate's Cove brand and constructing a commissary she could use to supply the franchisees' po'boys with their secret recipe. LaMarca considers herself blessed and believes the Pirate's Cove that some had feared would not be successful because it was "off the beaten path" was "what was meant to be."[42]

Except for Pass Christian Pet Care across the street, Jennifer Hendrick's Live Oak Animal Hospital is not anywhere near another business. What businesses there were around her veterinary clinic either never came back or moved east, closer to the downtown. It was quite a journey for Hendrick and her husband, accountant Scott Niolet. Besides having operated in a used rented trailer for years and then going through the hassle of building a new animal hospital, in the storm's aftermath Niolet took stock of his life. He had always been a songwriter, but he had never aggressively pursued recording. Now, with the pain associated with Katrina, he wrote—and a friend from his college days who was in New York produced—an album called *Clearing the Debris*. One of the songs, "Monday Afternoon Rain," and its accompanying music video received quite a bit of attention. But perhaps more importantly, after being together for many years, soon after the storm, Niolet proposed to Hendrick, and they were married, celebrating their eighth anniversary in the summer of 2014. As for Live Oak Animal Hospital, with a $700,000 investment in land and a new building, it took nine years to get the clinic back to where it was when the storm hit. Despite insurance costs for the new building that, according to Niolet, are 473 percent higher than before the storm, Hendrick is now to the point of hiring an associate to be able to handle all of her clients—exactly what she was doing when Katrina hit in August 2005.

Gulf Coast Pre-Stress (GCP) enjoyed four to five of the best years in the company's history after Hurricane Katrina, providing its pre-stress concrete products for rebuilding the infrastructure of Louisiana and Mississippi. At the peak, GCP had 350 employees working in its 110-acre facility in Pass Christian. Vice-president of sales Justin Yard said that even with the 2007 economic downturn, the company did well on contracts secured before the dip in the economy affected building. However, GCP is down to between 125 and 150 employees in 2014, with a decrease in demand starting in 2011 and continuing until today.

On weekends after the storm, the Jenkins brothers of Southern Printing and Silkscreening totally rebuilt three of their homes and renovated a fourth over a two-and-a-half-year period. Perry Jenkins says it was about 2008 when their business returned to close to pre-Katrina levels. The business is about 75 percent shirts, 15 to 20 percent printing and the rest making signs, which is largely seasonal, with elections being a major portion of the job. Jenkins says immediately after the storm some people urged him to move to Gulfport, where business would have picked up quicker. However, Perry and his brothers decided to bank on the long-term recovery of Pass Christian, having seen the city come back after Hurricane Camille. Business has been so good that the brothers have built a two-thousand-square-foot addition to provide more storage room. Meanwhile, Sazerac Square—a commercial development that grew from Martin Hardware and then Martin Plaza—remains the centerpiece of downtown. Adam Pace and his silent partners, Ben Puckett Sr. and Ben Puckett Jr., have had some tenants come and go, but they have been quickly replaced so that full occupancy has been the rule, not the exception. Without the creation of the "transitional" zone allowing for exceptions to the SmartCode requirements and tax breaks, those businesses may not have moved to Pass Christian's downtown.

After Hurricane Camille, Margaret Loesch's father sold their Scenic Drive home for $75,000. While Loesch went off to Hollywood and was involved in the creation and production of some of the most iconic shows in TV history, she always thought about reacquiring the Scenic Drive property. Hurricane Katrina afforded her the chance of a lifetime. One year after the coast's worst storm ever, the 625 East Beach Boulevard home sat with a shredded blue tarp on the roof, exposing it to the elements and causing it to deteriorate by the day. Because many contractors believed the home needed to be razed, Loesch negotiated to buy the property at the price of the land only. Hundreds of thousands of dollars later, admittedly after spending all of her children's inheritance, the home is now restored to pristine shape. In 2010, the home was 90 percent complete, and it was the host for the eightieth annual Valentine Silver Tea. It has been one of the highlights of the Pass Christian Historical Society's Tour of Homes. So the home that was originally built for the mayor of Gulfport in the mid-1800s, that had the attic converted into a second story in 1910, that required a significant makeover after the 1915 hurricane and that survived Hurricane Camille when others crumbled barely survived Hurricane Katrina and now rests in the capable hands of Margaret Loesch: "To me, Pass Christian is a state of mind as well as a place of beauty, and I wanted to do my part to help rebuild our town's beauty as well as share in our sense of community."[43]

The mayor and board of aldermen contemplated moving city hall, the city courthouse, the public library and police headquarters all to higher ground north in the city on Espy Avenue or elsewhere. However, if the city abandoned downtown, how could it justify trying to draw businesses and residents back? How could it justify lobbying the school district to remain at Church Avenue and Second Street or condemn the Biloxi Diocese of the Catholic Church for not rebuilding St. Paul's Church on Scenic? The common-sense solution prevailed in this case. City hall, the city court and the public library returned to essentially their exact footprint on what for 99 percent of the storms will be "high ground." The entire twenty-four-thousand-square-foot complex cost $6 million, which was covered by a grant, insurance and FEMA money. The combination Police Department and Emergency Operations Center built north on Espy Avenue near the eastern border between Pass Christian and Long Beach is designed to withstand the worst imaginable storm: 240-mile-per-hour sustained winds at thirty-two feet above sea level. The complex is completely self-sustainable for a minimum of seventy-two hours with a generator so powerful it provides electricity for business as usual, including air conditioning. The building includes an upstairs that can be used for bunks so firefighters and police officers have a place to stay if another devastating hurricane strikes. Finally, the complex includes what would be the equivalent to the president's "War Room," with computers and offices for the mayor and city attorney to use when the city is operating during a declared emergency. The cost of the police/emergency ops center was $4 million. In retrospect, Mayor McDermott concedes the need for the Emergency Operations Center to be on the highest ground possible but regrets not pushing to have the police station rebuilt in the downtown. However, Chief John Dubuisson calls the mayor and aldermen's decision to build the complex where and how they did "the best thing they ever did for the security of the city."[44] Dubuisson also applauds city officials for keeping the police force at the same numbers as before Katrina, despite a reduction in population. The police force stands at nineteen sworn officers and twenty part-time "on-call" police personnel.

Another positive from the storm's aftermath, that took nearly ten years to be fully realized, was the massive expansion to the east of the Pass Christian Harbor. The harbor had been partially rebuilt with a $2.3 million FEMA grant to get back functioning after the storm. Back in October 2006, Governor Haley Barbour pledged $25 million for a harbor expansion. But it

The new Pass Christian City Hall.

The interior of the new Pass Christian Library. *Courtesy of Tim Burkitt/FEMA, August 19, 2010.*

The new Pass Christian Police and Emergency Operations Center on Espy Avenue is built to withstand 240-mile-per-hour sustained winds.

took until December 2011 for the funding to be secured and permits issued so work could begin on tripling the old harbor's size. The $35 million project was christened on July 22, 2014, and includes 102 commercial boat slips and 62 recreational boat slips, as well as parking for 96 trucks/trailers and

215 spaces for automobiles. The money to build the new harbor came from a variety of sources, including the Mississippi Development Authority, the Coastal Impact Assistance Program and BP. The harbor is once again the home to the ten-thousand-square-foot Pass Christian Yacht Club (PCYC). Also located in the harbor, high up on pilings, is Shaggy's restaurant. Just as important, seafood vendors Pass Purchasing, Jerry Forte Seafood and Kimball's Seafood moved from the existing harbor to the new east side. The building of the harbor was not an easy process, like every other rebuild over the decade following Katrina, but it alleviated at least one major problem. Mayor Chipper McDermott described the Market Street south of Highway 90 entrance to the harbor as at times like the "Gaza Strip," with recreational boating interests—and specifically the PCYC—clashing with the commercial fishing industry needs. McDermott said the two sides "existed but did not co-exist."[45] At the christening, Governor Phil Bryant said that the coast had been in recovery, rebuilding and renewal for almost nine years, and the opening of the new expanded harbor meant it was finally growing again.

In May 2013, Jace R. Ponder acquired the *Gazebo Gazette* from founder and publisher Evelina Shmukler. At the time, Shmukler had reduced publication to every two weeks. By September, Ponder had achieved his first goal in purchasing the newspaper: returning to weekly publishing. That made the *Gazette* once again eligible to publish legal notices, which can be a steady stream of income. Second, Shmukler was sending copies of the *Gazette* to subscribers at standard postal rates. Ponder applied for and received a U.S. Post Office Periodical Permit, which cut in half the cost of mailing issues to newspaper subscribers. For those who subscribed to the paper, they noticed two changes shortly after Ponder took over. First, the flag or logo was changed in design, omitting the phrase, "A Newspaper for Residents and Friends of Pass Christian" to leave the door open for possible future expansion. He also changed to standardized columns and ad sizes and increased sports coverage. Ponder planned to run the newspaper for at least two years and then assess its future. Three months into ownership, he was breaking even, and in March 2014—just ten months after the sale—he received his first paycheck. The *Gazette* has about 550 subscribers and about 120 people purchase the paper from machines or local merchants each week. One year after acquiring the newspaper, Ponder is "happy" with the purchase, and the changes he made created what he considers a legitimate business model. In the fall of 2014, revenue was such that Ponder hired a part-time writer, making the paper no longer a one-man operation. The one worry Ponder has is a newspaper industry–wide worry: the demographics of *Gazette* readers skews older, and there is no guaranteed way to have an online version make money and survive.

Malcolm Jones returned to the position of city attorney after nearly a year serving as chief administrative assistant—essentially acting mayor—from September 2005 until August 2006. He remains the city attorney today. When Hurricane Katrina hit, Jones was city attorney and a relatively low-profile divorce lawyer. But during Pass Christian's darkest hour, when the elected mayor faltered, Jones stepped up and, by all accounts, made decisions that were critical to the city getting back on its feet. School board member Christopher Colby spoke for many in the city when he characterized Jones's performance in those days immediately following Hurricane Katrina as "brilliant."[46] Closing the city to residents seeking to return to assess their property for two weeks after the storm was extremely frustrating. Looking back, the dangers and difficulty associated with traveling in the devastated city and the desire to prevent looting justified the decision. Handing debris removal directly over to the Army Corps of Engineers and running temporary water and sewer lines on top of the ground to avoid the State Health Department from kicking people out of the remaining livable homes because of unsanitary conditions were two other decisions made by Jones in those chaotic days immediately following the hurricane that helped save the city.

Ward 3 alderman Anthony Hall and Mayor Chipper McDermott, who was an alderman before the storm, are two elected city officials who have served before, during and ever since Hurricane Katrina. Hall, by all accounts, survived and then thrived after Katrina. He survived physically, weathering the storm at the wastewater treatment plant, and he survived politically when redistricting after the 2010 census changed his ward from 60 percent African American and 40 percent white to about a fifty-fifty split. He has also thrived professionally, now managing seven wastewater treatment facilities for the Pearl River County Utility Authority, and as a public servant as chair of the Gulf Coast Community Action Agency, helping to rebuild head start centers throughout Harrison, Hancock, Stone and George Counties. As the senior member on the board of aldermen, he has served a diverse Ward 3 population, which includes 65 percent of the businesses in the city, as well as many of the city's working poor. Hall's one regret is that the city has not done a better job building facilities for the youth. For instance, the Boys & Girls Club gymnasium is shared with the school district, so city needs are third in priority. Meanwhile, Chipper McDermott moved seamlessly from alderman to mayor one year after the storm. When McDermott was a young man, his mother, Myrtle Spence McDermott, specifically advised him to "not get into this stuff [politics and government]." Myrtle's father—Chipper's grandfather—J.H. Spence, was the city's dentist and served as mayor for twenty-two straight years, eleven two-year terms in the early part of the twentieth century. Chipper's father, Leo, was a tax collector. Since elected to fill the unexpired term of Billy McDonald, McDermott has been reelected twice to four-year terms with the latest coming in the summer of 2013. Looking back on nearly a decade since the storm, McDermott believes the second year after Katrina was the hardest. McDermott said that in the first year, everyone worked day and night to get the city cleaned up and essential services such as sewer and water back. When that was accomplished, McDermott looked around his city, and there was nothing. Virtually everything—from streets and city buildings to schools, churches and businesses—had been wiped out. The city faced a daunting task. For all but that first year, McDermott has been mayor. He longs for the days before Katrina, when board of aldermen meetings would last twenty minutes, maximum, with virtually no controversial issues. Meanwhile, one of the last major projects directly tied to the Hurricane Katrina recovery, the expansion of the Pass Christian Harbor, was completed in 2014. The harbor is one of the reasons McDermott ran for reelection; he wanted to finish what he calls the largest building project in the city's history. When McDermott fills out his current term, he will have served eleven straight years as mayor, about half as long as his grandfather served. But one could argue that McDermott's years in office were the most critical in Pass Christian's long history.

Notes

Chapter 1

1. Johnson, "Service Assessment," 18.
2. This figure is from the 2002 U.S. census. Estimates are that the Pass may have had 6,800 or more by August 29, 2005.
3. John, Pass Christian Public School District, Executive Summary; City of Pass Christian Comprehensive Plan.
4. Huffman, "Mississippi Yearning," *Preservation*.
5. National Hurricane Center/National Oceanic and Atmospheric Administration, "RE-ANALYSIS." The National Hurricane Center in April 2014 downgraded Hurricane Camille from 190-mile-per-hour maximum peak winds to 175-mile-per-hour winds. This ruling came after researchers from the hurricane center and Florida International University reanalyzed original observations.
6. Schloegel, interview by James Pat Smith, August 14, 2008, USM KOHP.

Chapter 2

7. Lally, interview with Emily Finch, May 9, 2011, Hurricane Katrina Pass Road to the Future, USM Center for Oral History and Cultural Heritage, Hattiesburg, MS. (Referred to as USM KPRF from this point on.)
8. Knabb, Rhone and Brown, *Tropical Cyclone Report*, 11.

9. Ibid., 12.

10. Anthony, interview by Lawrence N. Strout, August 7, 2014.

11. Dubuisson, interview by Claire Gemmill and Jocelyn Wattam, February 19, 2009, USM KOHP.

12. Loesch, interview by Kira Burger and Laura Marshall, February 18, 2009, USM KOHP.

13. Malcolm Jones, e-mail communication with author, August 18, 2014.

14. Austin, interview with author, May 20, 2014.

15. Schloegel, USM KOHP.

16. James, interview with Elizabeth Smith, December 6, 2007, USM KPRF.

17. Peranich, interview with James Pat Smith, May 15, 2008, USM KOHP.

Chapter 3

18. Machalara and Shmukler, "Southern Ports Begin to Reopen," A12; Shmukler, "I Found My Dream Job on the Gulf Coast of Mississippi."

19. Burnett, interviewed by Bethany Mauer and Jackie Fry, February 19, 2009, USM KOHP.

20. *Gazebo Gazette*, January 13, 2006, 1.

21. Initially, debris on private property that threated the public health and welfare was removed without owner permission, under executive order.

22. *Gazebo Gazette*, "Editor's note," April 21, 2006, 11.

23. The final tally was twenty-eight dead.

24. For more information, Barbara Cloud of the University of Nevada wrote extensively about the Frontier Press.

Chapter 4

25. The Shmukler piece was labeled "A Letter from the Editor," but for the purposes of this book, we are calling it an "editorial."

26. Perkins, "Henderson Point Property."

Chapter 5

27. *Gazebo Gazette*, "The *Gazebo* Asks: What's Your Favorite Part, or Best Memory of Mardi Gras?" February 24, 2006, 5.

28. Penny J. Rodrique is married to the author of this book.
29. *Gazebo Gazette*, "Letter from the Editor: 'Why Not Do It Right?' Is Our New Motto, Too," May 25 and June 1, 2007, 26.
30. Bergeron, "Second Victim Recovered."
31. Southern Yacht Club was the first, and it moved to New Orleans.
32. Ken Austin, e-mail to author, July 14, 2014.
33. *Gazebo Gazette*, "St. Paul's Church to Be Turned into Community Center: New Parish Church Will Be Built North of City Limits," March 9, 2007, 1–2.
34. Ibid., "Bishop Says St. Paul Lawsuit Attacks Unity, Liberty of Church," May 11, 2007, 11.
35. McDermott, interviewed by James Pat Smith, March 14, 2008, USM KOHP.
36. Jace Ponder, "St. Paul Chapel Re-Opens," *Gazebo Gazette*, August 1, 2014, 1, 7.

Chapter 6

37. Burnett, interview with author, July 9, 2014.

Conclusion

38. Clary, "Mississippi Coast."
39. Marshall, interview with author, July 15, 2014.
40. *Clarion-Ledger*, "Pass Christian as Academic Powerhouse," May 18, 2014, http://www.clarionledger.com/story/news/2014/05/18/pass-christian-academic-powerhouse/9265581.
41. Garziano, interview with author, July 28, 2014.
42. LaMarca, interview with author, July 9, 2014.
43. Loesch, interview by Kira Burger and Laura Marshall, February 18, 2009, USM KOHP.
44. Dubuisson, interview with author, August 4, 2014.
45. Mayor Chipper McDermott, speech at Pass Christian Harbor christening, July 22, 2014.
46. Colby, interview by Katharine Wilson and Justine Baskey, February 18, 2009. USM KOHP.

BIBLIOGRAPHY

REPORTS AND REFERENCE SOURCES

Bergeron, Angelle. "Second Victim Recovered in Fatal Mississippi Bridge Form Collapse." *Engineering News Record*, June 18, 2007. enr.construction.com/news/transportation/archives/070618.asp.

Centers for Disease Control and Prevention (CDC) and the Agency for Toxic Substances and Disease Registry (ATSDR). "Response to Problem Drywall." www.atsdr.cdc.gov.

City of Pass Christian. Board of Aldermen. Minutes, 2006–2013.

City of Pass Christian Comprehensive Plan, revised October 26, 2006.

Clary, Gareth, "Mississippi Coast Has Three of the State's Fastest Growing Cities, According to New Census Data," Gulflive.com, May 22, 2014. blog.gulflive.com/mississippi-press-news/2014/05/mississippi_coast_has_3_of_sta.html.

Fitzpatrick, P., Y. Lau, S. Bhate, Yongzuo Li, Elizabeth Valenti, Bob Jacobsen and Joel Lawhead. *Storm Surge Issues of Hurricane Katrina*. GeoResources Institute, Mississippi State University. WorldWinds, Inc. URS. NVision Solutions, Inc. Twenty-first Conference on Hydrology, January 2007.

Huffman, Alan. "Mississippi Yearning: What Are the Chances of the Revived Gulf Coast Resembling Its Former Self," *Preservation*, September/October 2007. www.preservationnation.org/magazine/2007/september-october/mississippi-yearning.html#.

John, Beth. Pass Christian Public School District. Executive Summary, January 26, 2013.

Johnson, David L. "Service Assessment: Hurricane Katrina, August 23–31, 2005." National Hurricane Center/National Oceanic and Atmospheric Administration, June 2006.

Kieper, Margie. *Hurricane Katrina Storm Surge Part 10: Bay St. Louis to Pass Christian, MS*. Weather Underground. Sixteen-part series. www.wunderground.com.

Knabb, Richard D., Jamie R. Rhone and Daniel P. Brown. *Tropical Cyclone Report: Hurricane Katrina, 23–30 August 2005*. December 20, 2005 (updated September 14, 2011, for National Flood Insurance Program damage estimates and August 10, 2006, for tropical wave history, storm surge, tornadoes and fatalities).

Machalara, Daniel, and Evelina Shmukler. "Southern Ports Begin to Reopen." *Wall Street Journal*, September 8, 2005, A12.

National Hurricane Center/National Oceanic and Atmospheric Administration. "RE-ANALYSIS PF 1969's HURRICANE CAMILLE COMPLETE: Catastrophic Hurricane Now Ranks as Second Strongest on Record." April 1, 2014. www.nhc.noaa.gov/news/20140401_pa_reanalysisCamille.pdf.

Perkins, William H., Jr., "Henderson Point Property—Lead Story from January 22, 2009 Baptist Record: Developer Drops Henderson Point Offer." mbcb.org. www.mbcb.org/henderson.aspx.

Shmukler, Evelina. "I Found My Dream Job on the Gulf Coast of Mississippi." divinecaroline.com, July 2007. www.divinecaroline.com/article/22277/31950-found-dream-jobgulf-coast.

U.S. Consumer Product Safety Commission. Drywall Information Center. www.cpsc.gov.

ARCHIVES AND COLLECTIONS

University of Southern Mississippi Center for Oral History and Cultural Heritage, Hurricane Katrina Oral History Project (USM KOHP).
Burnett, Evelina (Shmukler)
Colby, Christopher
Dubuisson, John
LaMarca, Mike, Jr.
Loesch, Margaret
McDermott, Leo "Chipper" (2006, 2008)
Peranich, Diane C.
Schloegel, George A.

University of Southern Mississippi Center for Oral History and Cultural Heritage, Hurricane Katrina Pass Road to the Future (AmeriCorps, 2011) (USM KPRF).
Bang, Huey L.
Hall, Anthony
James, Kathryn "Sally"
Lally, Michael E., Jr.
McDermott, Leo "Chipper"

INTERVIEWS

Allison, Tommy
Anthony, Bruce
Austin, Ken
Burnett, Evelina [Shmukler]
Dubuisson, John
Garziano, Marsha
Hall, Anthony
Hendrick, Jennifer
Jenkins, Perry
Jones, Malcolm

LaMarca, Dawn
Marshall, George
McDermott, Leo "Chipper"
McGoey, Pete
Niolet, Scott
Pace, Adam
Peralta, Gene
Ponder, Jace
Smith, Carolyn
Yard, Justin

NEWSPAPERS

Biloxi (MS) Sun Herald
Jackson (MS) Clarion-Ledger
Pass Christian (MS) Gazebo Gazette, January 2006–August 2014.

ABOUT THE AUTHOR

D r. Lawrence N. Strout is a tenured associate professor in the Department of Communication at Mississippi State University in Starkville, Mississippi. Strout has a PhD in communication with an emphasis in media history from Florida State University in Tallahassee, Florida. Strout worked in commercial and public broadcasting for fourteen years before entering academia in 1990. He joined the faculty at Mississippi State University in August 2007. Strout has published numerous articles in scholarly journals and is the author of the book *Covering McCarthyism: How the* Christian Science Monitor *Handled Joseph R. McCarthy, 1950–1954* (Greenwood Press). Strout and his wife, Penny Rodrique, make their home in Pass Christian. Their daughter, son-in-law and granddaughter are Nicole, David and Lorelei Jordan, respectively, of Boston, Massachusetts.